Beer

O'Clock

CRAFT, CASK AND CULTURE

JANE PEYTON

summersdale

BEER O'CLOCK: CRAFT, CASK AND CULTURE

Summersdale Publishers Ltd
46 West Street
Chichester
West Sussex
PO19 1RP
UK

www.summersdale.com

Printed and bound in the Czech Republic

ISBN: 978-1-84953-476-5

Substantial discounts on bulk quantities of Summersdale books are available to corporations, professional associations and other organisations. For details contact Nicky Douglas by telephone: +44 (0) 1243 756902, fax: +44 (0) 1243 786300 or email: nicky@summersdale.com.

Contents

Introduction – Peerless Beer...5

The International Language of Beer..............................9

Beer's Early Years..13

Do the Brew..23

Time to Taste...35

Meet the Family – Beer Styles.....................................46

In the Mood – What to Drink?....................................102

Beer Hall of Fame...107

Looking Good – What Glassware?..............................113

A Little of What You Fancy Does You Good............122

Feast – Matching Beer with Food..............................130

Beers That Ruled the World..142

Great Brewing Nations of the World.........................157

Boozers in Britain – the Early Days.........................162

The Knowledge – Beer Trivia......................................170

Swotting for the Pub Quiz – Frequently Asked Questions and More...188

The Lingo – Glossary of Beer Terms.........................197

Acknowledgements...207

Dedicated to Sara Barton,
who made my dreams of brewing come true.

Introduction – Peerless Beer

Some people have humanitarians or sports stars as role models. Mine is a fearsome old battleaxe in a hairnet – Ena Sharples. She was the first person I ever saw drinking beer. I was six years old and can picture her now. There she would sit, with her friend Minnie Caldwell, in the snug of the Rovers Return, both of them enjoying a glass of milk stout as they gossiped about goings-on down Coronation Street.

A few years later as a teenager I ordered my first beer in a pub – Tetley Light Mild – and was instantly hooked. I enjoyed everything about the theatre of the pour – the landlady pulling the handpump and filling the glass, then presenting me with the most gorgeous vision, a pint of tan-coloured beer with a voluptuous foamy head. This was a Yorkshire pint – none of that 'no head on my beer, thank you very much' attitude that drinkers prefer in the south. It was love at first sight.

Back then my choice of pub was determined by whether it sold a good pint of Tetley cask beer. There were only four pubs in my home town of Skipton that did (out of more than twenty hostelries), so Friday night's pub crawl was fairly limited as most of the other boozers sold pasteurised beer and I knew that was the spawn of Satan. Today kegged beer is often superb but in the 1970s it was tasteless. When I went to university I abandoned my beery roots and started drinking cider for no other reason than it was cheap.

But the siren call of hops was too seductive and I had a thunderbolt moment in The Junction Inn, Otley with a pint of Timothy Taylor Landlord Ale. Goodbye cider, I was back with beer.

A few years later I moved to the USA. This was before the craft-beer revolution had spread far, and the beer was rubbish. The consolation was that I lived in California where the wine is excellent. Nine years later, when I returned to live in the UK, friends met me at Heathrow and we drove straight to the pub. I ordered a pint of London Pride and wept. I was home.

From then on I made up for lost time and had a great time visiting pubs and trying a plethora of beers. Several of the most popular beer styles currently brewed around the world originated in Blighty: India pale ale, pale ale, brown ale, mild, porter, stout and barley wine. How fortunate to be living in a country with such a diverse selection of beers to help reacquaint me with one of the things that put the 'great' in Britain.

I wrote several books, including one about pubs, and decided that the most fun I could have in my working life would be to set up a business where I could share with others my passion for beer. In order to have credibility as someone who knows what they are talking about, I studied with the Wine & Spirit Education Trust and the Beer Academy, from where my beer sommelier accreditation came.

In 2008 I founded the School of Booze, a corporate events company that specialises in beer, cider, wine and spirits tasting. Now I evangelise about beer to people wearing suits! One of the most satisfying aspects of my job is changing people's perceptions of beer. Many people do not realise that beer is more than just a pint of Pilsner, bitter or stout down the boozer, so when they get to taste a magnificent Imperial India Pale Ale or Trappist beer made by monks and experience its aroma, flavour and complexity they are invariably surprised.

Converting women to drink beer is a particular mission of mine. Beer is for everyone regardless of gender but many women feel it is not the drink for them. There are several reasons why, including the assumption that it is highly calorific (it's not) and that it tastes bitter. Some beers *are* bitter, but many are not. At this point of the beer conversation with women I pull out my trump card – a tangy Flanders red ale or a well-matured barley wine served in a tulip-shaped glass – neither of which is bitter-flavoured. Then I mention all the health benefits of a moderate consumption of beer, that the alcohol level of most beer is significantly lower than that of wine and spirits, and casually drop in the fact that beer was most likely invented by women. Quite often it works, and my tally of souls claimed for Ninkasi, goddess of beer, is rising.

I am devoted to good beer wherever it is made but there is no denying that British brewers make some of the best beer in the world. A quick note to the Aussies and Americans who say that Britons drink warm flat beer: compared to the artificially carbonated, ultra-chilled beers usually consumed in those countries, we do. And there's a reason. Depending on the style of ale, it is meant to be served at temperatures between 8 and 14 °C so the amazing aromas and flavours may be enjoyed to the full. Any colder and the beautiful character of the beer is muted – a person may as well drink fizzy iced water.

Ale is Britain's national drink and has been brewed here for millennia but, before hops were introduced into England in the fourteenth century, what people of the British Isles were drinking was a sweet libation lacking the bitterness that hops add to the brew. Beer was a hopped, bitter-flavoured beverage brewed in northern regions of continental Europe. Eventually ale and beer came to mean the same thing – an alcoholic drink made from water, malted cereal, hops and yeast. In this book I use both terms, ale and beer, interchangeably, unless I am referring to the era before hops made their debut in England (c.1362).

Ale was so important in England that it was mentioned in Magna Carta. Clause 35 states: 'There shall be standard measures of wine, ale, and corn throughout the kingdom.' If it was significant enough in the thirteenth century to include in a document that set out the freedoms and laws of the land, why have modern governments taken such an aggressive attitude towards beer when it comes to taxation? Britons pay 40 per cent of the beer tax collected in the European Union, and drinkers in London and South East England pay more beer tax than the entire country of Germany (the world's second-highest consumer of beer).

This book is an introduction to beer for people who like it and want to know more. It is a guide to the friendliest and most wholesome of all alcoholic libations – the drink for all moods and seasons. Exploring the diverse world of beer is great fun and, unlike any other alcoholic beverage, it is so packed full of nutrition and goodness that you'll be healthier at the end of the glass than you were when you started. During my research I especially enjoyed consulting these publications/blogs: *Amber, Gold & Black* by Martyn Cornell; *The Oxford Companion to Beer* edited by Garrett Oliver; Protz on Beer website by Roger Protz; Zythophile blog by Martyn Cornell.

So thank you for reading this tome. May beer always bring you joy. And if it doesn't, send it to me, please. I'll drink it.

The International Language of Beer

When Ludwig Zamenhof invented Esperanto in 1887, his goal was for humans to communicate in a common language so peace and international understanding could be fostered regardless of regional or national tongues. Perhaps he was not aware that a *lingua franca* already existed, and that it was called beer.

Oh beer, priceless gift to humanity, begetter of happiness, sociability and companionship. No wonder it is the world's number one favourite alcoholic beverage. And, astonishingly, it makes it as number three after water and tea as the most widely and oft-consumed drinks. Walk past a pub, inn, saloon, tavern, shebeen, bar, café, brasserie, bodega, lodge or boozer and look at the people who are having the most fun. What are they swigging? Beer, Bier, cerveja, biera, ビール, birra, bière, пиво, μπύρα, cerveza, 啤酒 of course!

Beer is the essential social beverage. There is nothing wrong with drinking it alone at home, but how much better does it taste when consumed in company? Beer is not the drink to turn to when in shock, or for drowning one's sorrows. Beer is playful. How many times does a quick beer after work end up hours later with people singing, arms round each other, as they profess unending friendship? It is beer goggles that make the world beautiful – not brandy goggles.

Picture the scene. A group of strangers are in a pub. One drinks whisky, another person a glass of wine; someone orders vodka.

Chances are they will remain strangers. Now take that same group and fill their glasses with beer. Within minutes they will be friends. Beer drinking encourages bonhomie. I have the satisfaction of observing this close up because I occasionally take visitors from all over the world around one of Britain's leading breweries. Some speak little or no English. Tour groups vary in their make-up: individuals, couples, sets of work colleagues. People are often shy and don't interact with each other beforehand. But in the bar afterwards when they start drinking the beer, something magical happens. Noise levels increase, laughter punctuates the air, and the atmosphere becomes very jolly as beer breaks down the barriers and everyone starts talking to one another – regardless of mother tongue. Then afterwards, as the visitors leave the bar, faces lit up with smiles, they invariably head to the nearest pub for more beer together with their new pals.

Try this experiment on your friends. Ask them what Spanish phrases they know. I bet you a fiver they will include – '*por favor*', '*gracias*' and '*dos cervezas, señor*'. 'Please', 'thank you' and how to order beer are the three absolutely necessary phrases for a happy holiday overseas.

On a recent trip to Zambia, where there are seventy-two tribal languages, I studied enough of the four main dialects to make myself understood when I ended up in a bar each night to drink Mosi, the local brew. In Zambia I realised that in addition to beer there is another international language – football. Luckily I am fluent in both, so now I have new mates in Mongu, Lusaka and Mufulira. It may have been Wayne Rooney who introduced us but it was beer that sealed our friendship.

BEER – A UNIVERSAL LANGUAGE

On trips overseas, if you do not speak the lingo, one word will suffice – beer. The root of the term 'beer' is believed to derive from the Latin verb *bibere* (to drink). The Old Norse word *bjórr*, Old High German *bior*, and Old English *beór* resemble the spelling and pronunciation of 'beer' but it is not clear whether this was the word for a fermented cereal beverage (beer), despite what the Oxford English Dictionary states. Some historic sources suggest that the word meant the more general term 'strong drink'.

The etymology of 'ale' is clearer – from Old English *ealu* via Old Norse *öl* and Saxon *alo*.

BEER LANGUAGE ROOTS

Different words for the amber nectar come from different language roots. Here's a sampling:

Afrikaans – *Bier*
Albanian – *Birra*
Bulgarian – *Бира* (pronounced *beer-a*)
Chinese – *Pi jiu*
Croatian – *Pivo*
Czech – *Pivo*
Danish – *Øl*
Dutch – *Bier*
Esperanto – *Biero*
Estonian – *Õlu*
Finnish – *Olut*

French – *Bière*
Gaelic (Irish) – *Beoir*
Gaelic (Scots) – *Leann*
German – *Bier*
Greek – *Μπύρα* (pronounced *beer-a*)
Hungarian – *Sör*
Italian – *Birra*
Japanese – ビール (pronounced *biiru*)
Korean – 맥주 (pronounced *maekju*)
Latvian – *Alus*
Norwegian – *Øl*
Polish – *Piwo*
Portuguese – *Cerjeva*
Romanian – *Bere*
Russian – *Пиво* (pronounced *pivo*)
Spanish – *Cerveza*
Swahili – *Pombe*
Swedish – *Øl*
Welsh – *Cwrw* (pronounced *coo-roo*)

Beer's Early Years

Modern beer contains water, malted barley, hops and yeast. Some of it may also have herbs, spices, fruit, vegetables, resin, chocolate, coffee and other flavourings in the brew. But the first beer was much more simple – water and cereal. Wouldn't you like to thank the person who invented it?

In fact, beer was discovered by accident in various parts of the world where cereal grew. The hypothesis is that grains being stored for food became damp and started to germinate in warm air. Germination converted starch in the grain to sugars that were fermented by airborne wild yeast spores. How that went from a handful of germinated seeds into something to drink is not clear. But humans are a curious species: how would we have known the pleasure of artichoke hearts if some inquisitive woman out gathering edible berries and plants had not wondered what was hidden inside those spiky leaves?

At some point it was discovered that if bread cakes made from germinated grains were added to water and heated, then left to cool, a few days later the result would be something tasty that triggered a gently mood-altering, intoxicating buzz. With a little experimentation others realised that if they chewed the cereal, spat it into a pan and then boiled it with water it made the process more effective. What they did not know was that the enzyme ptyalin in saliva would transform starch in the cereal to maltose and dextrose sugars that yeast would ferment, creating alcohol as a by-product.

Beer drinkers had advantages over those who abstained because fermentation increases the nutritional value of food and makes it easier to digest. All those vitamins, minerals, proteins, and amino acids in the barley made the brain grow larger. Fermented food contains *Lactobacillus acidophilus* microflora, which boost immune-system functions and maintain healthy intestines. Those who drank beer were vigorous, resilient, smarter, party people, and likely to live longer than those who did not. And how does nature reward the sturdier specimens? By making them more attractive to potential sexual partners. Meaning that beer drinkers were more likely to go forth and multiply. It is tempting to hypothesise that without beer and the evolutionary and health benefits it bestowed, perhaps humans would never have flourished, doomed instead to being dim-witted, puny, small-brained creatures. And karaoke might never have been invented.

Early beer bore no resemblance to what is brewed today, resembling instead murky pond water and, in the absence of hops, tasting sweet. It most likely had fruit and honey added to perk up the flavour. Any bitterness would have come from herbs and spices. Alcohol levels would not have been much higher than 5% ABV (alcohol by volume). Still, this nascent beer was so appealing that subsequent societies embraced it with a passion unmatched in the history of alcohol.

Beer became a staple of the diet, a wholesome foodstuff made at home for the whole family to drink throughout the day. It provided energy, nutrition, and was a safe source of water. As the saying goes, 'In wine there is wisdom, in beer there is strength, in water there is bacteria', and those invisible pathogens could cause myriad nasty ailments that, if they did not kill, made people very ill. Not only was beer essential for good physical health, it was also necessary for celebrations, communing with deities, and bonding with neighbours.

It is almost certain that the earliest brewers were women, because food and drink preparation was their domain. So Plato's often quoted phrase 'He was a wise man who invented beer' has lost something in translation. In Viking culture, the law stipulated that brewing equipment was the property of women, not men, and could not be sold or dispensed of without their permission. In the timescale of beer history, male brewers are a recent occurrence. Even now in tribal communities in the Amazon and parts of Africa it is women who make the beer and it would be very odd indeed for a male to be involved in anything other than drinking it.

It may be a surprise to people who consider beer to be a masculine drink that it has more feminine connections than any other alcoholic beverage. Not only were the first brewers women; the brewer uses the female part of the hop plant, and yeast cells that provide the alcohol are female. Throughout time different cultures around the world believed, in their creation myths, that beer was a gift to women from goddesses. The major deities of beer are female: Ama-Gestin, Ceres, Dea Latis, Hathor, Ninkasi, Mamasara, and Siduri – all worshipped in ancient societies by the act of communal beer drinking.

The earliest archaeological evidence of an alcoholic drink made from fermented cereal so far discovered was in a Neolithic village called

Jiahu in China dating back to *c.*7000 BC. Residue on clay pots was analysed and found to contain rice, honey and fruit. To date, the first sign of barley beer is on shards of clay jars found in a settlement in the Zagros Mountains of Iran dating from *c.* 3500 BC.

These finds do not reveal when beer was first brewed, however, because before earthenware containers, food and drink were stored in wooden vessels and animal skins, and being organic they would rot away over millennia leaving nothing for archaeologists to get their hands on. If, as some historians believe, beer and bread are inextricably linked, then according to finds of cereal flour at excavation sites in Italy, Russia, and the Czech Republic, humans were drinking beer at least thirty thousand years ago. Barley was a commonly grown cereal; the thing about barley is that it is rubbish for making bread with but brilliant for making beer. Our ancient ancestors knew their priorities. Make bread by all means, but only to crumble up and use as the starter for beer.

Beer lovers will no doubt support the theory by some anthropologists that the desire for beer and bread spurred the development of agriculture and civilisation. It happened first in the Fertile Crescent – Mesopotamia, the land between the Tigris and Euphrates rivers, an area that today covers Iraq, Syria, Turkey and parts of Iran. Hunter-gatherers were so enamoured of beer that they abandoned their nomadic lifestyle in order to plant barley and emmer (a type of wheat) and stay in one place to watch it grow. They formed permanent settlements and organised themselves to work together in communities, eventually developing all the associated trappings of society including law, bureaucracy, education, culture, religion, commerce and pubs. It's for this reason that the area is also known as the Cradle of Civilisation. And brewing and drinking beer was an essential part of it.

Beer-worship was an art that Sumerians, in southern Mesopotamia, excelled at. Beer was consumed by all ages, and by all strata of society, a major element of their cultural identity. Ninkasi was their goddess of seduction, fertility, the harvest and beer, and when Sumerians took a drink of the divine nectar, they uttered the toast 'Ninkasira' in gratitude. In order to prove their allegiance to Ninkasi, Sumerians gathered for great public feasts to drink prodigious amounts of beer and commune with her. There was no shame in drunkenness; indeed it was a spiritual state. Written language developed in Sumeria and the earliest known recorded recipe (for any food or drink), dating to 1800 BC, is contained in a poem called 'The Hymn to Ninkasi', a handy guide on how to make beer. A friendly greeting was 'May Ninkasi live with you, let her pour your beer everlasting.' Beer was the civilised drink and a person was not fully human or enlightened unless they drank it. And to think that some people today consider beer to be downmarket!

In Mesopotamian city-states such as Lagash and Babylon, regulations were drafted to enshrine in law the beer rations citizens were entitled to. Dire punishments were meted out to brewers and innkeepers who served short measures. Beware any foolhardy person who sold spoiled beer – they would be force-fed with it until death by asphyxiation.

Archaeological digs throughout the region have unearthed hundreds of clay tablets marked with cuneiform inscriptions that translate as recipes for beers with names such as *kassi* (black beer) and *kassig* (red beer). They demonstrate that beer was not just a recreational drink, but also medicine used for treating all manner of ailments. Today's drinker would turn their nose up at Mesopotamian beer because it had a thick gruel-like consistency with cereal husks and yeast cells floating around in it. That's why the drinking straw was invented in the Middle East, so people could enjoy a drink without getting a mouthful of detritus. Most used the hollow stem of a reed, but those with high status would have special decorated gold straws.

One of the greatest sayings ever uttered came from Ancient Egypt and translates roughly as 'the mouth of the perfectly contented man is filled with beer'. Beer was immensely important to Egyptians and it is likely that their appreciation of beer and skills at brewing came from Sumeria. Another popular Egyptian epigram was 'Do not cease to drink beer, to eat, to intoxicate thyself, to make love, and celebrate the good days'. Archaeological excavations near Hierakonpolis suggest that beer was brewed there from at least 3500 BC.

In Egypt, beer was made by dissolving bread cakes in water then mashing them in a reed basket and sieving the wort (sugary water) through the mesh into a clay jar; this was then sealed so yeast could ferment the sugars. Egyptians had a choice of different beers – 'thick beer', 'sweet beer', 'dark beer' – and some special brews called 'Beer of the Protector', and 'Beer of Truth'. Customers in Egyptian bars were served with a side dish of bitter plants such as skirret, or lupin flower seeds. When chewed and held in the cheek, this balanced the sweetness of the beer.

Today we know so much about beer in Egyptian society because they were such efficient documentarians. Of all foodstuffs mentioned in texts, the word for beer, 'hekt', was cited more often than any other. It was used to anoint newborns and as currency, tax, tributes to pharaohs from the provinces, medicine and food (the hieroglyph for 'meal' is a compound of those for bread and beer). Hieroglyphs and receipts exist to demonstrate its importance not just to the living but also in the afterlife. Brews with names such as 'Everlasting Beer', 'Beer That Does Not Sour' and 'Beer of Eternity' were placed in the tomb as offerings to tempt and intoxicate the gods so they would be kind to the soul of the deceased. Murals, including ones found in the tombs of pharaohs, show people drinking beer from a communal vessel through straws. The pharaoh controlled a significant amount of brewing, which turned out to be a shrewd move.

Beer's exalted position in the great civilisations of Mesopotamia and Egypt gave it cachet and its reputation grew. Trading routes were early information superhighways, and knowledge of the magical brew called 'beer' spread alongside commerce and conquest through the Mediterranean basin, along the Silk Road, and down the Great Rift Valley.

There is evidence dating back millennia of beer being drunk in far-flung corners of the world. In isolated regions, such as the Amazon, that had no communication with the outside world until relatively recently, rainforest dwellers brewed for centuries a style of beer called *chicha* from the sacred cereal, corn. Not only was it consumed for enjoyment, nutrition, bonding and rituals; in some tribes it was tradition to cremate the dead and then mix the ashes into *chicha* to keep the spirits within the community. This had an unforeseen additional benefit because the powdered bone acted as finings that clarified the beer.

It is most likely that the first beer on British shores was heather ale brewed in Scotland from at least 2000 BC by the pugnacious warrior-tribe known as the Picts. Heather roots often conceal fogg, a mildly hallucinogenic moss, so the ale would have packed a double whammy of intoxication. Today, Scottish brewing company Williams Brothers produce heather ale (brand name Fraoch, after the Gaelic word for heather), making it the world's oldest regularly brewed style of beer.

Over millennia, waves of invaders of Britain – Angles, Saxons, Jutes and Vikings – brought the habit of drinking their favourite libation with them, which served to reinforce native Britons' already long-held veneration for malt. Apart from the Romans with their wine, the Normans with their wine and cider (the Normans were originally Vikings but had long since adopted the drinking habits of the French), and the Dutch with their gin (the Dutch arrived when William of Orange overthrew King James II in 1688), for the natives it was beer, beer and more beer. Queen Victoria understood this need for beer amongst her subjects when she said, 'Give my people plenty of good strong beer and there will be no revolution amongst them.'

Evidence of beer in early continental Europe was discovered in Germany by archaeobotanist Dr Hans-Peter Stika. A site near Eberdingen-Hochdorf has Iron Age remains dating to 500 BC and he revealed a series of ditches there that contained thousands of grains of charred malted barley. This was a maltings in which the barley was germinated before fires were lit at the ends of the ditches to dry the grains. The beer would have had a smoky taste. Seeds from the stinking nightshade plant were also found and, added to the beer, they would have made it more intoxicating.

The desire for beer swept through Europe with the waves of Nordic and Germanic tribes who moved south and west in the first millennium AD, and, as the Christian church became increasingly powerful, it helped that the clergy was also enamoured of it.

Intoxication may have been a vice, but beer was considered a gift from God. It was brewed in monasteries to supply the daily ration for resident monks and nuns, as refreshment for travellers on pilgrimages, and to sell on a commercial basis. There was another reason why the church enthusiastically embraced beer – in order to win the souls of the populace, they had to accept people's source of enjoyment, and turn a blind eye to the habit of 'going for it' when presented with a mug of ale.

Perhaps the most significant factor in spreading a yearning for beer throughout the world was Britain's overseas trading outposts and colonies. With the founding of the East India Company in 1600, the first English settlement in Virginia in 1607, the penal colony in Australia's Botany Bay in 1788, and the arrival in Guyana in 1796, British influence reached across the continents, and so did its love of beer.

Of all alcoholic drinks, beer has perhaps the most vivid history, and has arguably contributed more positive gifts to humanity than any other – as a superfood, as a provider of medicine, nutrition and other health benefits, as a form of relaxation, conviviality, fun and pleasure. Ninkasira!

A HYMN TO NINKASI

Ninkasi was the Sumerian goddess of fertility, seduction, the harvest and beer. Her name means 'the lady who fills the mouth'. She was head brewer to the gods, and worshipped by humans for sharing her gift of beer with them.

The 'Hymn to Ninkasi' is a song of praise written on clay tablets in the ancient writing system of cuneiform by an unknown poet c.1800 BC. The words describe how to brew beer. Although it is likely that written language evolved in Sumeria, at the time most people would have been illiterate. But the 'Hymn to Ninkasi' with its rhythmic cadence and repetition would have been easy to learn. Very useful for brewers who were able to learn off by heart the instructions for brewing!

The text was translated into English in 1964 by Miguel Civil, Professor of Sumerology, Oriental Institute of the University of Chicago. These are the final two lines:

Ninkasi, you are the one who pours out the filtered beer of the collector vat,
It is the onrush of the Tigris and the Euphrates.

Do the Brew

On paper it looks so simple – combine water, malted cereal (malt) and hops together in a big pan and boil it for an hour or so. Cool the liquid and wait for wild yeast in the air to land, or add cultured yeast, so it ferments the sugars in the brew. Result – beer.

In practice, it is more complicated. It is easy to make bad beer and much trickier to make good beer. So the brewers who do make the good stuff are virtuosos. Brewing is alchemy. Each beer starts with a recipe when the brewer decides which malts to choose, what hop varieties to add, and alcohol strength of the ensuing alcohol. Brewing is like cooking but with bigger vessels and more washing-up.

Let's take a trip through the making of beer from field to firkin. It all starts with the cereal farmer who plants one or more of the popular varieties of malting barley (*Hordeum vulgare*) such as Optic, Maris Otter or Halcyon. After harvest, the cereal is sold to a maltster, who turns it into malt – a material for brewing with. There are several types of malt, with names such as pale ale, crystal, chocolate and black. Depending on the malts used by the brewer, the resulting beer varies in colour from straw, amber and brown to mahogany and black, and in flavours ranging from biscuit, bread, nuts or toffee to coffee and charred. Brewers can combine different malts for complexity of flavour and colour.

On brew day, the malt is milled into a rough powder called grist (hence the phrase 'grist for the mill') and this exposes the starch in

23

the grains. The grist is tipped into a vessel called a mash tun and sprayed with warm water, then mashed for up to three hours. At this stage it resembles porridge. Enzymes in the malt are activated and start working to convert the starch to simple sugars such as maltose. Water filters through the mash and collects sugar, colour and flavour, forming a liquid known as wort. It tastes like sweet biscuits and Ovaltine, is full of goodness and is known as 'brewers' breakfast'.

The grist is usually mashed twice; the first time sugar levels in the wort will be high, the second time they will be lower. Beer strength is determined by this level of fermentable sugars. A high concentration will make a strong, big-bodied beer (wort from the first mash), whereas low amounts of sugar will make a low-alcohol beer (wort from the second mash). Medium-strength beer is made by blending mash number one and mash number two.

The wort is transferred to the equivalent of a large pan known as a copper or brewing kettle. Hops are added for bitterness and aroma and any other ingredients such as herbs, spices and honey are thrown in and the wort is boiled. Some hops are used specifically for bitterness and others for aroma, but there are hops varietals that can be used for both. Bittering hops are added soon after the wort starts to boil. Aroma hops will be poured into the copper towards the end of the brewing session so the volatile essential oils they contain do not vaporise. If the beer is to have a particularly hoppy character the brewer will 'dry hop' the beer – this means hops are added in the fermenting and maturation tanks and maybe even into the cask, where they steep into the brew. Good brewing is about balance of ingredients.

Before the brew is sent off to a fermenting tank it is cooled and the spent hops and proteins from the cereal are extracted – this mixture, known as trub, often ends up back on a farm as animal feed, just as the malt does after it has been used for brewing.

Once the brew arrives in the fermenting tank, the magic really starts; this is when the nectar is transformed to become beer. Yeast is added to start the dramatic process of fermentation. For it to work effectively, optimal temperature, oxygen and sugar levels are essential. Up to 34 billion yeast cells are required to make one pint of beer. Those identical clones double in number in ninety minutes, so the brewer ends up with much more yeast than they started with.

The trillions of excess yeast cells may end up on a farm as pig food, in the health food store as vitamin B (Brewer's Yeast) tablets, as fertiliser, in the food chain as flavouring, or, most famously, as Marmite.

Depending on the beer style, it will be allowed to ferment for between five and fourteen days. It is then matured or 'conditioned': three to seven days is the normal conditioning period for ale, and three to eight weeks is normal for premium lagers (though most mass-produced lagers are conditioned for a fraction of that time). This maturation process is known as 'lagering' from the German verb '*lagern*', meaning 'to store', and during this time complex and desirable flavours develop and undesirable compounds such as sulphur and diacetyl (tastes like butterscotch) are purged.

Finally the beer is ready to be packaged and delivered to a pub, club, shop or elsewhere. Then thirsty hordes do what humans have done for millennia – have a drink with a friend.

YOU SCRATCH MY BACK...

It may sound as though the brewer is a slave to yeast and to a certain extent that is the case. But in reality it is a symbiotic relationship because the brewer supplies the yeast with what it requires to go forth and multiply. Yeast is temperamental and demands comfortable working conditions. If these are met and maintained, individual yeast cells commence a big sugary love-in as they reproduce by cloning themselves. As they do so, they voraciously consume the sugars and nutrients in the brew, thereby creating alcohol, carbon dioxide, heat, and hundreds of aroma and flavour compounds.

Yeast reproduces asexually so that means there are no male yeast spores. All those clones are sisters, another good reason for not thinking of beer-drinking as a predominantly male pastime!

Ingredients

Each of the four main ingredients of beer (water, malt, hops and yeast) influences to varying degrees what the beer smells, tastes and feels like. Let us look at each in turn:

Water

Not all water is equal when it comes to brewing, because the water's contribution depends on the geology of the rocks it travels through and on the amount and type of salts suspended in its solution. These will influence taste and mouthfeel, and therefore the style of beer that the water is suitable for. Some brewers have their own local source of fresh water, a well or a spring, and that gives their beers so-called *terroir*, but most brewers have to rely on the local mains water, known in brewing parlance as 'town liquor'. If local (fresh or mains) water is just not suitable, brewers can add or subtract salts to fit the beer they want to brew.

HOW THE MINERAL COMPOSITION OF WATER AFFECTS BEER

Very soft water: as this is low in mineral salts, it is ideal for Pilsner lagers because it showcases the sharp bitterness of the hops and the sweet biscuit of the malt. (This is the water of Pilsen in the Czech Republic, from where the name of the beer style derives.)

Medium-hard water: this is high in calcium chloride, so it is good for making sweeter beers such as mild and brown ale (medium-hard is typical of Britain's West Midlands).

Hard water: with high levels of calcium sulphate and bicarbonates, this is perfect for dry beers such as bitter and India pale ale, because it highlights the hops (typical of the water found in Burton-upon-Trent in Staffordshire).

Very hard water: high in calcium bicarbonate, which is very good at extracting colour from the malt, and therefore used to make stout. The water of Dublin in Ireland is very hard and therefore ideal for the production of Guinness. London water is also full of calcium bicarbonate, and consequently two of the world's greatest dark beers, porter and stout, were first brewed in the city.

Malt

Malt, as we have seen, is malted cereal – the backbone of beer which provides the sugars for yeast to ferment and transform to alcohol. It also gives beer its colour, some flavours, its body, foam, head retention and nutrition. Beer is sometimes called 'liquid bread' and malt is the reason. British malting barley is renowned throughout the world and is not only used to make beer and whisky in Britain; it is also exported to brewers and distillers overseas. The temperate maritime climate and soils of Britain unite to grow the highest-quality and most-flavoursome barley. Uniquely, British farmers can harvest two crops a year – winter and spring varieties.

While barley malt is the preferred cereal for beer with excellent flavour, because it has high amounts of starch and enzymes that convert that starch to sugars such as maltose, in fact anything containing starch can be used to make beer. Other grains, such as wheat, contain enzymes but they are not as effective, so even a wheat beer will contain a high percentage of barley malt for the super-active enzymes. Give thanks for those enzymes, because without them the saccharification would have to happen by chewing the cereal. Human saliva contains amylase (also known as ptyalin) and this starts the process of digestion in which complex carbohydrates are broken down to simple sugars. In some parts of the world, such as the Amazon rainforest, maize beer (*chicha*) is still made communally by the women of the village, who sit masticating the cereal before spitting it into a dish and rolling it into little balls to dry in the sun. These are dropped into a pan and water is added, brought to the boil and then cooled. Fermentation by airborne wild yeast begins and *voila*! – the sacred libation of *chicha* is ready to drink.

SOMETHING FISHY GOING ON?

A common adulteration of beer in eighteenth-century London was a material called hard multum derived from the crushed seeds of an Indian climbing plant *Anamirta cocculus*. Known in English as fish berry, the seeds were poisonous and used in India to stupefy fish in the water so they would float to the surface and be caught easily. Hard multum increased the effects of intoxication in beer so the brewer could save money by using less expensive malt in the brew, malt being the source of alcohol, thereby increasing profits.

Hops

O *Humulus lupulus*, wolf in plant's clothing, how do I love thee – those vibrant aromas and flavours you offer, that refreshing bitterness you impart? Known in English as the hop, it is a herbaceous perennial climbing plant and the flowers from the female plant are harvested for brewing because they contain an oily resin (lupulin), which gives aroma, flavour and bitterness to beer. Hops are also antibacterial so they act as a natural preservative. In botanical terms *Humulus lupulus* is related to the cannabis plant but the active ingredient (tetrahydrocannabinol) that provides the psychotropic effect is not present in hops.

Just as the grape gives specific characteristics to wine, so the hop varietal does to beer, with flavours including citrus, herbal, grassy, fruity, floral, woody, peppery, spicy and earthy. A brewer will choose a hop depending on its properties and the style of beer being produced. India pale ale, for instance, demands highly aromatic and bitter hops, whereas imperial Russian stout will include bittering hops but hop aroma is not normally important.

Without the bitterness from hops, beer would taste like digestive biscuits due to the malt sugars in the barley. If that sounds appealing, try drinking a pint of something that resembles Horlicks. Then another one. No? Me neither.

Yeast

Meet *Saccharomyces cerevisiae*, the magician that converts malted cereal sugars to alcohol through the process of fermentation. It is a species of yeast – a single-celled fungus that floats around in the air looking for its favourite food: sugar. Even non-drinkers are probably familiar with *S. cerevisiae* because it parks itself on the peel of fruit, waiting for the skin to rot so it can drill through to gorge on that luscious juice, which is then fermented by the yeast to alcohol. Don't throw away rotting fruit, eat it – and you'll know how the earliest humans felt when they discovered that it gave them a buzz.

There are hundreds of strains of *S. cerevisiae* and brewers can play around with yeast and let it mutate or blend with other strains until they have their own chimera. Such yeast cannot be purchased, therefore it really is priceless. It will contribute a unique character to the beer and is so precious to the brewer that it is stored in a food technology laboratory called a yeast bank in a different location to the brewery, where it is frozen in liquid nitrogen at -196 °C. People in white coats care for the yeast and make sure it is healthy and happy. This means the brewer always has a secure source of yeast in case the brewery burns down.

There are three tribes in the beer family – ale, lager and Lambic – and the major difference between them is the strain of yeast the brewer uses for fermentation. Ale brewers employ *S. cerevisiae* which ferments quickly at temperatures of 16–20 °C, adding fruity aroma and flavour to the beer. Brewers of lager-style beers use a hybrid yeast strain called *Saccharomyces pastorianus*, evolved from *S. cerevisiae* and *Saccharomyces bayanus*. It ferments slowly at temperatures of 10–15 °C and gives the beer a crisp body by fermenting more of the sugars in the wort. Less aroma or flavour comes from lager yeast than from ale yeast. With lager, the geology of the water (low on mineral salts) is also a factor that contributes to a light body.

Lambic brewers do not use cultured yeast; instead they open the window and allow airborne spores to float in, land in open fermenting tanks and spontaneously ferment the brew. Some of those spores are a strain of yeast called *Brettanomyces* and, along with other microflora that live in the local atmosphere, give the beer a tangy and sour character more akin to cider or wine.

With ale and Lambic, up to half the aroma and flavour in the beer comes from yeast (less so with lager) and quite often it is these characters that drinkers respond to, and the reason why they might prefer one brewer's beer over another's.

Packaging

Once the beer is ready, it needs to be delivered to the customer. The brewer has a number of packaging options – cask, keg, bottle or can.

Cask ale

Cask-conditioned ale (aka real ale) is unfiltered and unpasteurised so the yeast is still active in the beer, converting the remaining sugars into alcohol and carbon dioxide. As it ferments and matures in the cask, complex flavours develop. In the pub cellar, cooled to temperatures of 11–13 °C, the publican taps open the cask and inserts a plug called a 'spile' which helps to maintain the natural CO_2 in order to keep the beer in good condition. Before it is ready to serve, yeast and protein cells in suspension need to settle into the belly of the cask with the help of finings that are used to clarify the beer, e.g. isinglass finings.

The publican samples the beer to ensure it is at its best and then a plastic pipe is attached to the cask through which the beer is drawn into a glass by the pulling of the handpump on the bar. Because cask ale is 'live', the shelf life is limited. Once a cask has been tapped the beer starts to deteriorate after three days. After a week or so, a drinker may notice a vinegary smell. If so, send the beer back and ask for something else because a pub should not be serving stale beer. It will not physically harm the drinker, but it will offend the palate.

Cask ale is the most natural way of drinking beer and it represents the epitome of the brewer's craft.

WHAT IS ISINGLASS?

Isinglass is a collagen substance derived from the swim bladders of fish (the balloon that keeps the fish afloat). It is very effective in clarifying cask ale and quickly helps to drag yeast cells and other solids to the bottom of the vessel. Although drinkers do not consume the isinglass, strict vegans will avoid cask ale as it has been in contact with an animal product. Ancient societies would have noticed that when they stored beer or wine in animal stomachs or bladders it had greater clarity when served, but no one knows who first thought of experimenting with material from inside a fish. For centuries, sturgeon was the preferred source of isinglass but those fish are endangered now and many other large species are used. The Chinese food industry uses more isinglass (as a source of gelatin) than brewers do.

Kegged beer

With this method, after the beer has fermented and matured in the brewery it is filtered and pasteurised, carbonated with carbon dioxide and often nitrogen, and then packed into a pressurised container called a keg. This beer is now stable and does not deteriorate as quickly as cask ale does; unlike cask ale, it is low-maintenance and needs little attention. To serve it, a tap is opened on the bar and gas pressure forces the beer through plastic pipes to the glass. Once opened, the shelf life of kegged beer is five to six weeks.

Bottle and canned beer

Just like kegged beer, this is filtered and pasteurised then carbonated. After bottling or canning, the beer lasts for thirty-six to fifty-two weeks. The colour of glass bottle can affect flavour because if light gets through to the beer it can change a compound in the hops, such that they give off a pungent aroma described by some people as cheesy, or like cat wee. This phenomenon is called 'lightstruck' and can be prevented by using brown glass. Clear and green glass offers no protection against the light, although brewers can buy modified hops that no longer contain the problem substance.

Bottle-conditioned beer

Live beer is bottled and, just before the bottle is sealed, a dose of yeast is added. This starts a secondary fermentation. After a few weeks the yeast goes dormant and drops to the bottom of the bottle as cloudy sediment. Some people prefer not to drink the last dregs of the beer where all the sleeping yeast cells have gathered. Waste of beer! As the beer matures, complex flavours develop. Try this experiment with a case of bottle-conditioned ale above 7% ABV: drink a bottle each Christmas and make a note of the character of the beer. It will change from year to year.

How long does bottle-conditioned beer last for? By European Union law the label must state a 'best before' date, usually one to two years after bottling, but, with strong beers above 8% ABV, ignore the date, because they often do not reach their peak for two to three years. At the time the label says you should have consumed it, the beer is still maturing and improving with age. One of my favourite bottle-conditioned beers was brewed in 1999 and I recently found two bottles of it in my secret stash. Joy! I opened one and took a sip. It was the equivalent of liquid Christmas cake – a massive dried fruit extravaganza that reminded me more of Madeira wine than beer. The hop bitterness had completely gone and it was a juicy fruity marvel. The second bottle did not last long either.

Time to Taste

Tasting beer properly does not just involve taking a swig and swallowing. It starts as soon as a person decides to have a drink – even before the order has been placed at the bar – with that delicious anticipation and mental decision of 'What am I in the mood for?'

Because beer is an everyday drink, many people do not realise how multilayered it is. So grab a glass of your favourite libation and let's do a tutored tasting workshop.

In most people, all the senses are engaged when tasting beer, whether they notice them all or not, and it all contributes to the enjoyment:

Hearing: The sound of the beer sloshing from the handpump at the bar, or the schlozzle of carbonation as a bottled beer is poured into a glass.

Sight: The beer's appearance: glassware, colour, clarity, and foam head. Fickle creatures that humans are, we judge what we see within three seconds. First impressions count!

Smell: Without aroma we would not taste our food and drink properly, because the brain registers 80 per cent of flavour through olfactory cells in the nose. When we take a mouthful of food or drink, the aromas are released and dissolve into the nasal cavity from within the mouth. Then six million receptors send messages to the brain about the flavours. When a person has a blocked nose they cannot properly taste their food, because they cannot *smell* it. To test the power of the nose, pour a glass of Scotch whisky and give it a sniff or two then taste it. It might have honey, heather and spice characteristics. Now hold the nose and take another sip. All the subtlety is gone and it may taste of salt and little else.

Aroma, therefore, gives clues on what we are about to taste. The smell of something can be a warning as to whether it will be good for us, or harmful. People check if milk or meat is off by smelling it. An inviting aroma is crucial, otherwise we won't take the next step and taste it. But some unfortunate people who have an inability to smell (a condition called anosmia) will not taste their beer as others do.

Ideally beer should be swirled to release those vital aromas. The shape of glass is important for retaining them – try a wine or brandy glass, tulip or snifter, and do not fill it to the brim. Hold it up to the light and admire the colour, then twirl the beer. Take two or three sniffs and try to identify the aromas. If it just smells like beer and you are unable to discern anything else, worry not – practice makes perfect!

Taste: Now it is time to take a sip. Let the beer cover all areas of the tongue to stimulate the approximately seven thousand taste buds that will recognise sour, sweet, salt, bitter, and umami (savoury) flavours. The tongue is compartmentalised into taste zones. Salt is mainly registered at the tip of the tongue, sweet at the front and front sides, sour along the sides, umami in most areas, and bitterness at the back. People with no sense of taste suffer from a condition known as ageusia.

As the beer warms in the mouth, aromas are released and travel up into the nose where the olfactory cells send messages to the brain. When the beer is swallowed the bitter aftertaste registers. This is called the 'finish' or the 'hang' and means how long the bitterness and other flavours stay on the tongue. Bitterness is part of the beer's design and is one reason why it must always be swallowed – no spittoons allowed! The other reason is that, according to the beer police, it is an offence to throw beer away! And even undrinkable beer has its uses: to attract slugs and snails in the garden so they can be moved next door to the nasty neighbour's rockery; to water the plants with; and as a hair rinse – all that vitamin B in beer is good for the Barnet (for readers unfamiliar with Cockney rhyming slang, 'Barnet fair' equals hair).

Women are more sensitive to bitterness than men are, while men are more sensitive to sweetness. There may be an evolutionary factor here; when humans were nomadic hunter-gatherers, the women would search for plant food and taste-test it in the field. Bitterness is often a warning signal of toxins and so such plants would be avoided. When I ask female non-beer drinkers why they do not like it, the answer is invariably that it is too bitter for them. The good news is that not all beer is bitter – so, dear reader, your mission, if you choose to accept it, is to enlighten your non-beer-drinking associates and introduce them to German wheat, Belgian Lambic or aged English barley wine, none of which has discernible bitterness. And what happens to beer ambassadors who make successful conversions? They go to beer heaven.

If on the first sip a beer does not appeal, try, try again because three is the magic number. The brain may get used to it if tasted slowly. The first sip might be 'urgh, it's disgusting'; second sip 'hmm, maybe it's not that bad'; and third sip 'I love you'.

Mouthfeel: This combines with all the other sensory experiences to enhance enjoyment of the beer. It includes:

Temperature: too cold and the aromas and flavours are muted and the more bitter it will taste; too warm is not ideal either (see below for more)

Texture: smooth, creamy, chewy or grainy

Body: light, thin, medium or full

Astringency: a drying mouthfeel (such as a bone-dry Irish stout)

Carbonation: flat or tingly; carbonation increases acidity and concentrates bitterness, so the higher the carbonation, the dryer and more bitter the beer will seem.

The factors that impact upon the flavours that eventually arrive in your mouth are alcohol content, serving temperature, the aromas and flavours that derive from the ingredients, the malting process, and the selected hops. Let us consider each in turn:

Alcohol

Tastes and smells sweet. In beers over 5% ABV it becomes noticeable. Alcohol has a warming effect and the higher the ABV level, the sweeter and smoother the beer will be, because the ABV level balances astringency and bitterness.

Serving temperature

Depending on where in the world beer is served, the temperature might range from 12 °C for British cask-conditioned ale to what may feel like absolute zero for lager in Australia or the USA. Temperature influences our perception of the beer because lower temperatures mute aroma and reduce sensitivity to flavour and mouthfeel. But in the end it comes down to personal preference. These are the guidelines for a variety of beer styles:

Imperial Russian stout: 14 °C

British and American ales, Trappist and abbey beers, bières de garde: 12–13 °C

Summer and golden ales: 10 °C

Altbier, Bock, Pilsner, Helles, Kölsch, Lambic, witbier, Weizenbier: 6–8 °C

Super-chilled lager: 0–4 °C

Aromas and flavours

Beer can be extraordinarily complex, and tasting experts have identified hundreds of aromas and flavours in different styles around the world. Here are examples of some of the characteristics that you might notice when you drink beer:

From water: Clean, dry, mineral, soft, sulphur.

From hops: Aniseed, berries, botanic, earthy, elderflower, floral, gooseberry, grapefruit, grapes, grassy, herbal, lemon, lychee, orange, orchard fruit, passion fruit, peppery, pine, spice, stone fruit, woody.

From malt: Barley sugar, biscuit, brown bread, burnt, caramel, cereal, chocolate, coffee, honey, liquorice, nuts, raisins, roasted, smoked, toast, tobacco, toffee, treacle.

From yeast: Bubblegum, banana, pear, clove, orange, peach, plum, pineapple, strawberry, spice, pepper.

Malting process

Brewers have quite the choice of cereals for making beer with: barley, corn, millet, oats, quinoa, rice, rye, sorghum and wheat. But barley is the best. Even if a beer has oats and rye in it, the recipe will also include barley because it contains high levels of the essential enzymes required to bring out the sugars. Whichever cereal or cereals are chosen, they must be malted, because unmalted 'raw' cereal cannot be fermented.

Malting, as we have seen, involves steeping the cereal grain in water. For approximately three days, the seeds germinate and the natural enzymes contained within alter the cereal starch into a soft powdery substance. To arrest the germination process, the maltster heats the cereal to dry it out. Depending on the temperature used in the heating process, the malt will range between lightly toasted to heavily roasted, each with distinct flavours and colours. The malt is now ready to be sold to a brewer.

Here is a list of the most commonly used malts and the qualities they give to beer:

Lager or Pilsner malt: Flavour: mild biscuit, maltiness. Colour: straw. Used as a base for many beers and mixed with coloured malts. On its own as a single malt it is good for making lager and blonde ale.

Pale ale malt: Flavour: biscuit, grainy, bread, nuts, maltiness. Colour: straw. Used as a base for many beers and on its own is good for making blonde ale.

Cara malt: Flavour: sweet, caramel. Colour: golden. Used for lager and golden ale.

Munich malt: Flavour: sweet biscuit. Colour: amber. Used for dark lager.

Amber malt: Flavour: baked biscuit. Colour: amber. Used for brown ale and mild.

Crystal malt: Flavour: caramel, toffee, nutty, roasted. Colour: copper. Used for bitter and ruby ale.

Brown malt: Flavour: dry, caramel. Colour: brown. Used for mild and porter.

Chocolate malt: Flavour: coffee, chocolate, roasted. Colour: mahogany. Used for dark mild, stout and porter.

Black malt: Flavour: dry, smoky, charred. Colour: black. Used for stout.

Wheat malt: Flavour: biscuit. Colour: straw. Used for wheat beer and blonde ale.

Roasted unmalted barley: brewers of stout often use roasted barley in addition to dark malts. It adds a charred, dry, bitter character to the beer that is typical of Irish dry stout such as Guinness.

Hops

A brewer is like a chef, combining ingredients to create something sublime. Think of hops, therefore, as the herbs and spices in the brewer's cupboard. Without them the brew would be bland. Depending on the varietal, the hop will have specific qualities of bitterness, aroma and flavour. And what an incredible choice the brewer has.

Hops are grown in several temperate countries such as Australia, Britain, Czech Republic, Germany, New Zealand and the USA. In Britain the main commercial growing areas are Herefordshire, Worcestershire and Kent, whose hops are celebrated for their complex, aromatic and flavoursome qualities, but without being 'in your face' as some New World hops can be. They give British brewed beers a highly drinkable quality. Although only 2 per cent of the world's hop output is grown in Britain, hop farmers produce twenty varietals, with new ones in development. Contrast that with Germany, where 37 per cent of hops used in world brewing are grown – yet there are twenty to twenty-five varietals. So for such a comparatively small yield, British hops are exceptionally diverse. *Terroir* (the influence of climate, soil and local conditions) is also a factor with hops. For instance, a Cascade hop grown in its home – the USA – will be bolder than when cultivated in the UK. Thank cloud cover and a lack of sun for the subtlety of British hops!

Ready for some hop worship? Meet the superstars of the brewing scene and their main characteristics:

Hop varietals:

Admiral (Britain): pine, orange

Amarillo (American): citrus, flowery

Beata (Britain): honey, apricot, almond

Bobek (Slovenia): pine, lemon, floral

Boudicea (Britain): spicy, light floral

Bramling Cross (Britain): spicy, blackcurrant

Cascade (USA): lychee, floral, grapefruit

Celeia (Slovenia): lemon, lime, floral

Challenger (Britain): spicy, cedar, green tea

Chinook (USA): grapefruit, citrus, pine

Citra (America): lychee, pineapple, mango, papaya, lime

Columbus (USA): sherbet, black pepper, liquorice

East Kent Goldings (Britain): sweet spicy citrus, fruit, floral. This varietal is registered under European Union law as having Protected Designation of Origin status and only hop farmers in east Kent are permitted to grow it.

El Dorado (American): tropical fruit, pear, watermelon, citrus

Endeavour (Britain): citrus, blackcurrant, spice

Fuggle (Britain): grassy, minty, earthy

Goldings: (Britain): spicy, honey, earthy (this is a slightly different varietal to East Kent Goldings)

Galaxy (Australia): passion fruit, peaches

Hersbrucker (Germany): floral, herbal

Liberty (USA): spicy, lemon, citrus

Magnum (Germany): resinous, herbal, pine

Mittelfrüh (Germany): herbal, floral, grassy

Motueka (New Zealand): lemon, lime, floral

Nelson Sauvin (New Zealand): elderflower, gooseberry, lychee, mango

Northdown (Britain): spicy, cedar, pine

Pacific Gem (New Zealand): dark fruit, oaky

Pacific Jade (New Zealand): herbal, lemon zest, black pepper

Phoenix (Britain): chocolate, spicy, molasses

Pilgrim (Britain): spicy, citrus, pears

Pilot (Britain): spicy, lemon, marmalade

Pioneer (Britain): cedar, grapefruit, herbal

Pride of Ringwood (Australia): cedar, oak, herbal

Progress (Britain): floral, mint

Saaz (Czech Republic): earthy, herbal, floral

Sorachi Ace (Japan): lemon, coconut

Southern Cross (New Zealand): lemon peel, pine needles

Target (Britain): pine, cedar, liquorice

Tettnang (Germany): earthy, herbal, floral

Topaz (Australia): spicy, resin, fruitcake

Wakatu (New Zealand): floral, zesty lime, vanilla

Williamette (USA): blackcurrant, spicy, floral

In Britain hops are harvested in September and quickly dried in kilns to prevent them from rotting, and so they can be stored until the following year's crop is ready. Green hops (also known as fresh hops) can be used for an even more pronounced hop character but brewing then needs to happen within forty-eight hours of picking. Some brewers drive down to a hop garden (as they are called in Kent) or hop yard (Herefordshire and Worcestershire) to collect the freshly harvested green hops and rush them quickly to their brewery, being careful not to fall asleep at the wheel because hops have a pronounced soporific effect – hence their use in herbal sleeping tablets!

British hop farms are noted for not practising gender apartheid when it comes to the male and female hop plants. Although only the female plant is used for brewing, the males are not banished the way they are in US and German hop fields. This leads the hop farms in the latter to being jokingly referred to as 'nunneries'.

Meet the Family – Beer Styles

Think of beer styles as dog breeds – some are pure-bred, others crossed, quite a few are mongrels. It is the same with beer. A stout, for instance, is easy to define and for a drinker to recognise, but a golden ale is trickier, blurring the characteristics of blonde ale and pale ale. And then there are the oxymorons such as black IPA (IPA stands for India pale ale), and the new craft brewers who create hybrids because they have a bold and adventurous attitude to brewing; they often make 'bigger' beers with higher alcohol levels and, when hops are a feature, intense bitterness that makes some of their beers hard to categorise. Beer styles are a guide when deciding what to buy, in the same way that knowledge of grape varietals helps a person choose the wine they like.

This chapter is a guide to the world's major beer styles, with typical characteristics, ideal temperature for serving, appropriate glassware, relevant food matches, and type of yeast used. The latter is a pointer to which category the beer falls into ('ale', 'lager' or 'Lambic'): warm top-fermenting yeast is used to produce ale; cold bottom-fermenting yeast is used to produce lager; and wild, spontaneous-fermenting yeast is used to produce Lambic.

Abbey

Characteristics: golden to dark brown in colour. Aromatic, full-flavoured, fruity, caramel, spicy and complex with low to medium bitterness.

Abbey beers originated in Belgium, the term being coined to describe beers brewed in the style of Trappist ales, but not necessarily in monasteries by monks. Abbey is not a specific style and covers a range of beers from light to dark, dry to sweet, that have in common the characteristics above. Their distinctive flavour and aroma traits derive from Belgian yeast strains. Some abbey beers are labelled as 'Dubbel' (double – refers to alcohol strength and intensity of flavour); these are russet brown with a gentle bitterness, toffee sweetness and taste of dried fruit, usually with strengths around 6–8% ABV. Others are labelled as 'Tripel' (triple); these are usually golden and range from 7% to 10% ABV. They often have a sweet malt, fruity base and subtle bitterness. 'Quadrupel' is less common than the others, and such beers deliver a fruity, figgy thump on the nose as well as alcohol levels of around 14% ABV.

Abbey beer labels may feature monks or other ecclesiastical motifs but it does not guarantee that they were brewed by men or women of the cloth. In Germany, abbey beers are known as Kloster (cloister) beers.

Drink this if you like big malt and aromatic yeast-dominant beers.

Good examples: Brune by Leffe (Leuven, Belgium); Ambiorix Dubbel by Brouwerij Slaghmuylder (Ninove, Belgium); Tripel by Affligem (Opwijk, Belgium); Gulden Draak 9000 Quadruple by Brouwerij Van Steenberge (Ertvelde, Belgium)

Glassware: chalice

Serving temperature: 8–13 °C

Yeast: warm-fermenting

Typical alcohol by volume (ABV): 6–14%

What food? Abbey beers are extraordinarily versatile food beers and match well with bacon dishes, spare ribs, asparagus, liver, charcuterie, roast duck, game, roast goose, goulash, mushroom dishes, cheese pasta dishes, pâté, rabbit, ratatouille, roast lamb, salami, sausages, truffles, turkey, venison.

Altbier

Characteristics: amber to dark brown in colour. Malty, nutty, toasty, gently spiced, fruity, crisp and medium-bodied with medium bitterness.

Altbier originated in Düsseldorf, Germany. The word 'alt' means old, which may refer to the old style of beer before the Pilsner lagers of Bavaria and Bohemia began to dominate. Altbiers are matured in tanks at cool temperatures for up to eight weeks and this creates mellow, highly drinkable beers.

Drink this if you like malty, easy-drinking beers.

Glassware: narrow cylindrical glass (called a *Stange* in Germany)

Good examples: Alt by Uerige Obergärige Hausbrauerei (Düsseldorf, Germany); Alt by Brauerei Schlösser (Düsseldorf, Germany)

Serving temperature: 8–12 °C

Yeast: warm-fermenting

Typical ABV: 4–5%

What food? Roast beef, burgers, burritos, roast and fried chicken, cheese on toast, macaroni cheese, meatloaf, roast pork, sausages, steak, Thai food.

Barley wine

Characteristics: amber to copper in colour. Malty, toasty, fruity, bittersweet, complex, high-alcohol, full-bodied.

Barley wines are big complex beers where the alcohol is apparent as soon as the glass goes to the lips. They are highly aromatic, usually with a combination of intense fruitiness and hops. There are enough hops in the beer to counteract the sweetness of the malt and high alcohol content. American barley wine often differs from traditional English versions by being highly hopped and heftier in alcohol content. English barley wine balances malt with hops.

Barley wine originated in England in the mid eighteenth century when war with France interrupted the import of *le vin*. Brewers experimented with pale malts and created strong beers aged in wooden barrels for months, even years. The beers had fruity vinous characteristics and were an alternative at the table to wine.

These beers are meant for sipping from an elegant glass, and at their best they can send the drinker into a rhapsody – especially when paired with cheese. Brewers rarely produce these beers for sale in a cask; they are invariably sold in bottles and can age into something remarkable.

Drink this if you like big, complex sipping beers with an orchard full of fruit and a warm alcoholic glow.

Glassware: snifter (also called a 'balloon')

Good examples: Benedictus by Durham Brewery (Bowburn, Co. Durham); Harvest Ale by J. W. Lees (Manchester)

Serving temperature: 14–16 °C

Yeast: warm-fermenting

Typical ABV: 7–12%

What food? Cheese, especially strong English varieties such as Lincolnshire Poacher, Cheddar, Stilton; Christmas cake, crème brûlée, lasagne, macaroni cheese, ploughman's lunch, sausage and mash, shepherd's pie, Sunday roast.

Belgian strong dark ale

Characteristics: amber to garnet in colour. Aromatic, spicy, malty, toasty, fruity, caramel, medium to big body, low bitterness.

These beers tend to be dry on the palate with virtually no hop character. When poured they have a generous, pillowy foam head. Some resemble abbey and Trappist beers due to the use of distinctive Belgian yeasts.

Drink this if you like spicy, sweet, malty beers.

Glassware: tulip

Good examples: Gulden Draak by Brouwerij Van Steenberge (Ertvelde, Belgium); McChouffe by Brasserie d'Achouffe (Achouffe, Belgium)

Serving temperature: 8–13 °C

Yeast: warm-fermenting

Typical ABV: 6–12%

What food? Much like the abbey and Trappist beers, these match well with bacon dishes, spare ribs, asparagus, liver, cassoulet, charcuterie, roast duck, game, roast goose, goulash, mushroom dishes, cheese pasta dishes, pâté, rabbit, ratatouille, roast lamb, salami, sausages, truffles, turkey, venison.

Belgian strong pale ale

Characteristics: straw to golden in colour. Aromatic, spicy, malty, biscuit, medium to big body, medium bitterness.

When poured these have a big foamy head and this leads to complex rounded flavours. Hops are balanced with the malts for a tangy bitterness. The alcohol is often apparent on the nose. Despite the high alcohol these beers can be dangerously drinkable. The spiciness comes from aromatic Belgian yeasts.

Drink this if you want a refreshing, spicy beer with a beautifully balanced combination of malts and hops.

Glassware: tulip

Good Examples: Duvel by Brouwerij Duvel Moortgat (Breendonk-Puurs, Belgium); Delirium Tremens by Brouwerij Huyghe (Melle, Belgium)

Serving temperature: 5–10 °C

Yeast: warm-fermenting

Typical ABV: 5–10%

What food? Charcuterie, chicken, Chinese, fish stew, hummus, Indian (mild), paella, pasta dishes (vegetarian), ratatouille, risotto, seafood, white fish.

Berliner Weissbier

Characteristics: pale and cloudy. Tart, refreshing, lemony citrus, mildly sour, light to medium body, low bitterness.

These wheat beers are quenching, effervescent and low-alcohol. They used to be brewed only within Berlin city limits but several American brewers now produce this style. The sourness comes from a lactobacillus culture (artificially produced bacteria) combined with the yeast.

Drink this if you want a refreshing wheat beer.

Glassware: weizen

Good examples: Berliner Kindl Weisse by Berliner Kindl Brauerei (Berlin, Germany); Freigeist Abraxxxas by Gasthaus-Brauerei Braustelle (Cologne-Ehrenfeld, Germany)

Serving temperature: 5–7 °C

Yeast: warm-fermenting

Typical ABV: 3–6%

What food? Chinese, egg dishes such as omelette and quiche, fish cakes, Indian (mild), hummus, risotto, salad, white fish.

Bière de garde

Characteristics: amber to copper in colour. Toasted malt, caramel sweetness, earthy, light spicy fruit, medium body, low to medium bitterness.

These beers originated in France and Flanders. The name means 'beer for keeping', so in the days before refrigeration they were made in cooler months, as beer spoiled in warm weather. The best examples are bottle-conditioned and come in Champagne-style bottles sealed with corks. They are usually made with warm-fermenting yeasts, although cool-fermented filtered versions exist, but as an exception rather than a rule.

Drink this if you want a complex, earthy, caramel beer.

Glassware: snifter or tulip

Good examples: Jenlain Bière de Garde by Brasserie Duyck (Jenlain, France); Jessenhofke Bière de Garde by De Proefbrouwerij (Kuringen-Hasselt, Belgium)

Serving temperature: 11–13 °C

Yeast: warm-fermenting (usually)

Typical ABV: 6–8%

What food? Casseroles, charcuterie, cheese dishes, fish stew, game, olives, pâté, rice and beans, Sunday roast (including chicken, duck and turkey).

Bitter

Characteristics: pale golden to dark amber in colour. Well-hopped, biscuity malt, often with caramel, citrus or floral aroma, high bitterness.

Beer is Britain's national drink and cask-conditioned (or real ale) bitter with no discernible carbonation is the classic style that most personifies British brewing and pubs in the late twentieth and early twenty-first centuries. Ask for a pint of bitter in a British pub and you might be served with a pale, highly hopped brew, or a dark amber, fruity caramel beer – light-, medium- or full-bodied. Bitter is a wide-ranging style but what they should all have in common is assertive flavour, even if the alcohol level is low. The secret is hops, and British brewers are renowned for creating flavoursome session beers with relatively low alcohol. 'Bitter' is a nickname dating from the mid nineteenth century to distinguish the beer from other popular beers of the time – porter and lightly hopped mild. Within the style there are sub-styles: 'Ordinary' (does not refer to its quality!) is 3–4% ABV, 'Best' is 4–5% ABV and 'Special' is 5–6% ABV. 'Light Ale' is sometimes used to describe lower-alcohol bottled versions of bitter.

Drink this if you want a flavoursome pint with medium to high bitterness.

Glassware: English pint, or dimpled barrel

Good examples: Sussex Best by Harveys (Lewes, Sussex); Landlord by Timothy Taylor (Keighley, West Yorkshire)

Serving temperature: 11–13 °C

Yeast: warm-fermenting

Typical ABV: 3–6%

What food? Barbeque, burgers, cheese dishes, classic pub grub – pies, sausage and mash, fish and chips, lasagne, macaroni cheese, ploughman's, sandwiches, shepherd's pie, steak, Sunday roast.

Blonde ale

Characteristics: pale straw to golden in colour. Crisp, bready, lightly fruity, light body, medium bitterness.

These are usually easy-drinking beers with a biscuity malt undertone. The hop character is more likely to be as aroma rather than bitterness. This style can be confusing, as some brewers describe their beers as 'Blonde' or 'Golden Ales' when they are more like pale ales with the associated bitter hop characteristics.

Drink this if you want a good session beer that is light and easy drinking.

Glassware: English pint, or dimpled barrel

Good examples: Brewers Gold by Crouch Vale (South Woodham Ferrers, Essex); Discovery by Fuller's (London)

Serving temperature: 6–10 °C

Yeast: warm-fermenting

Typical ABV: 3.5–5.5%

What food? Fish and chips, grilled chicken, grilled white fish, haloumi, hummus, pizza, ploughman's.

Bock

Characteristics: tawny to dark brown in colour. Slightly sweet, biscuity malt, toffee, full-bodied with floral or fruity notes, moderate bitterness.

This is a medieval German style of beer, believed to have originated in a town called Einbeck, which may explain its name. The word 'bock' denotes a strong beer up to a blockbuster 14% ABV. There are a number of bock beers depending on the season or your own mood. Maibock, sometimes known as Hellerbock or Hellesbock, is a spring beer to be drunk in May and June, between the cold winter, when a Doppelbock ('doppel' means double in German) or Eisbock keeps you warm, and the hot summer, when visits to the *Biergartens* to drink cooling helles or Pilsners become mandatory. Weizenbock (wheat beers) are perfect year round. Eisbocks have high ABVs (9–15%), because a percentage of water in the beer is frozen and removed, leaving concentrated alcohol. These beers are full-bodied with a fruity spice flavour, plenty of malt and virtually no bitterness.

Drink this depending on the weather and your mood. If you like the 'full malty', this is the beer for you. If you are a 'hophead', try something else.

Glassware: *stein* or *weizen*

Good examples: Salvator Doppelbock by Paulaner Brauerei (Munich, Germany); Weizenbock by Allgäuer Brauhaus (Kempten, Germany); Hofbräu Maibock by Staatliches Hofbräuhaus (Munich, Germany); Schneider Aventinus Weizen-Eisbock by Weissbierbrauerei G. Schneider & Sohn (Kelheim, Germany)

Serving temperature: 11–16 °C

Yeast: cool-fermenting

Typical ABV: 6–14%

What food?

Doppelbock: Bacon dishes, baked potato with cheese, cheese pasta, chilli con carne, crème brûlée, game, goulash, lentil dishes, roasted duck, mushroom dishes, nuts, pâté.

Weizenbock: Banana desserts, Chinese, Indian (mild), roast goose, steak tartare, trout, tuna steak.

Maibock: Cheese fondue, ham dishes, Indian (spicy), paella.

Eisbock: this is a meal in itself but goes well with nutty cheese (such as Lincolnshire Poacher), pecan pie and treacle tart.

Brown ale

Characteristics: copper to mahogany in colour. Toffee, coffee, nutty, fruity, sweetish, medium body, low bitterness.

This lightly hopped, fruity, easy-drinking beer is an old English style dating from at least the medieval era. Think of porter and mild as convivial cousins of brown ale. In the land of its birth, brown ale has gone out of fashion and few good examples of the style are brewed, but across the pond, American craft brewers give it a reverence that is missing in Blighty. Newcastle 'Newky' Brown has many enthusiastic fans in the USA and is perceived and marketed as quite a posh English beer. Yes!

Drink this to keep the style alive! Also if you are in the mood for a nutty, caramel, malty and lightly hopped beer.

Glassware: English pint, or dimpled barrel

Good examples: 09/02 Nut Brown Ale by Brew by Numbers (London); Hazelnut Brown Nectar by Rogue Ales (Newport, Oregon, USA)

Serving temperature: 6–10 °C

Yeast: warm-fermenting

Typical ABV: 3.5–6%

What food? Barbeque, burgers, bean burritos, chilli beans and rice, full English breakfast, hummus, kebabs, nuts, ploughman's, roast chicken, Sunday roast, steak, satay chicken or vegetables, sausage and mash, shepherd's pie (also works with vegetarian version), stew, tomato pasta dishes.

Brut des Flandres, aka bière brut or bière de Champagne

Characteristics: pale straw in colour. Bready, floral, apples, light body, lively effervescence, low bitterness.

If you know anyone who says they don't like beer, serve them one of these in a flute and wait for their reaction. This is where beer meets Champagne because although it is brewed as ale, it is finished like sparkling wine. After brewing, the beer goes into a Champagne-style bottle and is reseeded with yeast then laid horizontal on a rack and aged in a cool cellar for up to a year. Throughout maturation the bottles are rotated (aka 'riddled') to encourage the yeast to settle in the neck. When the beer is fully matured, the bottle neck is chilled so the yeast freezes and is expelled in a plug of ice. Then the bottle is sealed with a Champagne cork and metal wire basket (called a *muselet*).

Who says beer cannot be elegant? These beers are special indeed, and far too good to smash against the hull of a launching ship!

Drink this instead of Champagne. It is a good aperitif. If light spritzy beers sound appealing then this is the one.

Glassware: flute

Good examples: DeuS Brut des Flandres by Brouwerij Bosteels (Buggenhout, Belgium); Malheur Bière Brut by Brouwerij De Landtsheer (Buggenhout, Belgium)

Serving temperature: 6–10 °C

Yeast: warm-fermenting

Typical ABV: 11–12%

What food? Fish cakes, seafood, smoked salmon, sushi.

Burton ale

Characteristics: Dark copper in colour. Fruity, nutty, malty, caramel sweetness, well hopped, big body.

This style originated in the mid eighteenth century in Burton-upon-Trent, Staffordshire. Before India pale ale grew to dominate in Burton's breweries a century later, this was *the* international beer, exported in particular to Russia and the Baltic states. Well hopped and with a high alcohol content, it improves with age. Few British brewers still market this beer as 'Burton Ale' but several make it and call it 'strong' or 'old' ale. Fuller's revived one of their 1930s recipes for a limited-edition beer called 'Old Burton Extra' and they also regularly brew 1845, voted by CAMRA (Campaign for Real Ale) as the 'Bottle-conditioned Beer of the Decade 2000–2010'; although it is labelled as 'strong ale', it fits all the characteristics of a Burton ale. Some American craft brewers are keeping the style alive by producing versions of this heritage beer.

Drink this as a winter warmer or when you are in the mood for big flavour and body.

Glassware: chalice

Good examples: 1845 by Fuller's (London); Owd Roger by Marston's (Burton-upon-Trent, Staffordshire)

Serving temperature: 8–13 °C

Yeast: warm-fermenting

Typical ABV: 6–8%

What food? Hearty food such as strong cheese, game, sausage and mash, Sunday roast, stew, venison.

Dinner ale

Characteristics: pale amber in colour. Light-bodied, gentle bitterness, easy-drinking.

Before water was safe to drink, people consumed prodigious amounts of beer on a daily basis. Every meal was accompanied by beer, and all members of the family drank it, from the working classes to the aristocrats. Another name for dinner ale was 'family' ale and some brewers would deliver casks to local houses for consumption at home. When screw-top bottles were invented in London in 1879, dinner ale was sold in bottles for the table. Although it was largely pale ale, some brewers made 'Dinner Stout'. Dinner beers went out of fashion with changing tastes, beer tax increases, and shortage of materials during World War One. Today a handful of breweries in Britain, the USA and Australia produce this style of beer.

Drink this if you like light, gently hopped, uncomplicated and refreshing beers.

Glassware: snifter or wine glass

Good examples: Dinner Ale by Ilkley Brewery (Ilkley, West Yorkshire); Harvesters' Ale by Badger Ales (Blandford St Mary, Dorset)

Serving temperature: 8–10 °C

Yeast: warm-fermenting

Typical ABV: 3–4%

What food? Everything! The beer is intended to refresh the palate whilst eating.

Doppelbock

See the entry for 'Bock'

Dortmunder lager

Characteristics: pale golden in colour. Grassy, grainy, bready, delicate aromas and flavours, light body, medium bitterness.

These beers originated in the city of Dortmund and are similar to German Pilsners with a biscuity undertow, delicate, clean character and dry mouthfeel. Dortmunders are no longer produced as widely in Germany as they are in the USA, however; American craft brewers are keeping this style alive.

Drink this if you like light, clean, uncomplicated German Pilsner.

Glassware: lager

Good examples: Dortmunder Union Export by Dortmunder Union Brauerei (Dortmund, Germany); Dortmunder Gold by Great Lakes (Cleveland, Ohio, USA)

Serving temperature: 5–7 °C

Yeast: cool-fermenting

Typical ABV: 4–7%

What food? Caesar salad, cheese on toast, corn on the cob, egg dishes, fish and chips, grilled white fish, leek and potato pie, sushi, Welsh rarebit.

Dubbel

See the entries for 'Abbey' and 'Trappist' beers. The Flemish word *dubbel* (double) refers to alcohol strength (usually around 7–8% ABV).

Dunkel

Characteristics: ruby to mahogany in colour. Nuts, toffee, malty, bready, chocolate, light to medium body, low to medium bitterness.

Dunkel means 'dark' in German and this everyday easy-drinking lager-style beer is a native of Munich. Dunkels tend to be rich, very malty (but not sweet), with little apparent hop character.

Drink this if you are a malty maven; not a beer for hop lovers.

Glassware: dimpled barrel or stein

Good examples: Augustiner Dunkel by Augustiner-Bräu (Munich, Germany); Aufsesser Dunkel by Brauereigasthof Rothenbach Sonnenhof (Aufsess, Germany)

Serving temperature: 6–10 °C

Yeast: cool-fermenting

Typical ABV: 4–7%

What food? Cheese dishes, Chinese, French onion soup, hummus, leek and potato pie, lentil dishes, meatballs, meatloaf, mushroom dishes, roasted chicken, roasted pork, shepherd's pie, stews, sausages.

Dunkelweizen

See the entry for 'Weizen'.

Eisbock

See the entry for 'Bock'.

English strong ale

Characteristics: amber to mahogany in colour. Caramel, malty, fruity, full body, medium to high bitterness.

In the family of beer this rich and complex style is a middle child, somewhere between a pale ale and a barley wine. They are flavoursome big beers for sipping rather than supping.

Drink this for a robust full-flavoured malty brew.

Glassware: chalice or tulip

Good examples: 1698 by Shepherd Neame (Faversham, Kent); Broadside by Adnams (Southwold, Suffolk)

Serving temperature: 8–13 °C

Yeast: warm-fermenting

Typical ABV: 5–8%

What food? Cheese, lasagne, pies, pizza, ploughman's, sausage and mash, shepherd's pie, steak, Sunday roast.

Extra special (or strong) bitter (ESB)

Characteristics: Dark copper in colour. Rich malt, toasty, fruity, marmalade, full body, medium to high bitterness.

ESB or 'extra special bitter' was introduced by Fuller, Smith & Turner in 1971 and is a thrice Champion Beer of Britain. The style is a bigger, smoother, more complex version of a classic malty English bitter. No British brewers apart from Fuller's are permitted to call their stronger bitters 'ESB' but in America there is no such rule, so many brewers produce their own versions of this style.

Drink this for a full-flavoured, full-bodied, balanced beer where neither the hops nor malts dominate the other.

Glassware: English pint, or chalice

Good example: ESB by Fuller's (London); AleSmith Anvil ESB by AleSmith Brewing Company (San Diego, California, USA)

Serving temperature: 5–10 °C

Yeast: warm-fermenting

Typical ABV: 5–6%

What food? Barbeque, burgers, cheese dishes, lasagne, pies, pizza, ploughman's, shepherd's pie, sausage and mash, steak, Sunday roast.

Faro

Characteristics: pale, sweetly tart, medium body, no bitterness.

This is a style of Lambic beer (see 'Lambic' entry below for a definition) that is sweetened with the addition of syrup and quite often spiced with orange peel and coriander seeds. The tartness underpins the sweetness and allows acidity to come through on the palate, so the beer is still refreshing.

Drink this to explore the funky world of Lambic beers but without the shock of a tart gueuze (see entry below).

Glassware: snifter or tulip

Good examples: Drie Fonteinen Faro by Brouwerij Drie Fonteinen (Beersel, Belgium); Lindemans Faro Lambic by Brouwerij Lindemans (St Pieters Leeuw-Vlezenbeek, Belgium)

Serving temperature: 8–10 °C

Yeast: wild-fermenting

Typical ABV: 4–6%

What food? Chinese (sweet and sour), roast duck, sweetish cheese such as mascarpone.

Flanders red ale

Characteristics: ruby in colour. Sharp, tangy, fruity, medium body, no bitterness.

When is a beer not a beer as we know it? When it is a Flanders red ale? This style of beer (sometimes called Flemish red beer) is a speciality of Flanders in Belgium, and one of the most singular alcoholic drinks. It is assertively tart and complex and owes its sourness to a combination of yeast strains and other microflora used to ferment the beer (cultured yeast and wild microflora such as *Brettanomyces*). Brewers will age red ale in oak barrels for eighteen to twenty-four months and then blend younger with older beers from different casks. Try this test – serve it to a friend in a wine glass without telling them it is beer and ask them to identify what it is. They might say 'sherry' or 'red wine' and when you reveal that it is beer the reaction is often disbelief.

Drink this if you like the idea of balsamic vinegar in beer form. And if you don't – still try it for the experience of drinking a sour, complex, refreshing, extraordinary beer.

Glassware: snifter or tulip

Good examples: Duchesse De Bourgogne by Verhaeghe (Vichte, West-Vlaanderen, Belgium); Grand Cru by Rodenbach (Roeselare, Belgium)

Serving temperature: 8–10 °C

Yeast: warm-fermenting

Typical ABV: 4–8%

What food? Avocado, ceviche, Chinese (sweet and sour), creamy cheese such as goat's cheese or Vignotte, grilled sardines, moules marinière, oysters, pâté.

Frambozen (aka Framboise)

Characteristics: cloudy raspberry-pink colour. Raspberry, vanilla, sour-sweet flavours, medium body, no bitterness.

Frambozen means raspberry in Flemish and this Belgian style of beer includes macerated raspberries in the recipe. The base beer is normally Lambic (see entry below) and a skilful brewer will blend different-aged Lambics to create a spritzy tart beer with a hint of sweetness. Some brewers make cheaper versions with brown ale rather than Lambic and add fruit syrup – these tend to be sweeter and cloying. Authentic Lambic Frambozens are fermented with wild yeast and other microflora.

Drink this for a refreshing, sour-sweet, juicy, fruity experience.

Glassware: flute, snifter or tulip

Good examples: Boon Frambozenlambik by Brouwerij F. Boon (Lembeek, Belgium); Cantillon Frambozenlambik by Cantillon (Brussels, Belgium)

Serving temperature: 6–10 °C

Yeast: wild-fermenting

Typical ABV: 3.5–6%

What food? Ceviche, creamy cheese, Chinese (sweet and sour), chocolate puddings, coffee puddings, crème brûlée, melon, oysters, pâté.

Golden ale

Characteristics: rich golden in colour. Zesty, biscuit, fruity, floral, dry, light to medium body, medium to high bitterness.

This beer is the love child of pale and blonde ale – a sunny, golden brew with plenty of hops to give a lasting bitterness.

Drink this when in the mood for a sharp, refreshing, zesty beer, particularly in a summery beer garden.

Glassware: English pint, or dimpled barrel

Good examples: Decadence by Brewster's Brewing Company (Grantham, Lincolnshire); Brentwood Gold by Brentwood Brewing Company (Brentwood, Essex)

Serving temperature: 8–10 °C

Yeast: warm-fermenting

Typical ABV: 4–6%

What food? Avocado, chicken, creamy cheese, falafel, fish and chips, Indian (spicy), satay, grilled or smoked salmon, sushi.

Gose

Characteristics: pale straw in colour and cloudy in clarity. Tart, gently spiced, subtly fruity, medium body, low bitterness.

This old German style of unfiltered wheat beer hails from a town called Goslar where it was first brewed in the early eighteenth century. Brewers in Leipzig adopted and popularised it. They are crisp, dry, lemony beers with a spicy tang from ground coriander seeds, and although the addition of salt adds sharpness, the taste is not overly salty. It is no longer a mainstream beer but a number of German and American brewers keep the style alive. The beer is made with warm-fermenting yeast, with lactic acid bacteria added during fermentation for the sour character.

Drink this if you are in the mood for a light, refreshing, tart beer and to keep the style alive.

Glassware: dimpled barrel or stein

Good examples: Bayerischer Bahnhof Original Leipziger Gose by Gasthaus & Gosebrauerei Bayerischer Bahnhof (Leipzig, Germany); Triumph Gose by Triumph Brewing Company (Princeton, New Jersey, USA)

Serving temperature: 8–10 °C

Yeast: warm-fermenting

Typical ABV: 4–6%

What food? Caesar salad, ceviche, chowder, egg dishes such as omelette, quiche, fish cakes, grilled white fish.

Gueuze

Characteristics: pale golden, cloudy, dry, spritzy, earthy, sour fruit, dry, tart, light to medium body, no bitterness.

Gueuze is a style of Lambic (see entry below) made by blending young and older beers, then bottling them where a secondary fermentation takes place. The style originated in Belgium but experimental brewers in other countries are increasingly producing their versions of this extraordinary beer.

Drink this for a surprise and to appreciate the huge diversity of beer. For people who enjoy a challenge with a tart and acidic beer. Not for maltheads or hopheads!

Glassware: flute or tumbler

Good examples: Cantillon Lou Pepe Gueuze by Brasserie Cantillon (Brussels, Belgium); Girardin Gueuze Black Label by Brouwerij Girardin (Sint Ulriks-Kapelle, Belgium)

Serving temperature: 10–13 °C

Yeast: wild-fermenting

Typical ABV: 3.5–6%

What food? Avocado, cheese (especially goat's and blue), fish cakes, pâté, oily fish such as mackerel and salmon, shellfish.

Hefeweizen

See the entry below for 'Weizen'.

Helles (aka Hell)

Characteristics: pale golden in colour. Herbal, bready, refreshing, light body, low bitterness.

In German the word 'helles' means pale or bright and this lager style that originated in Munich fits that description. When Pilsner beers from the Czech Republic gained popularity in the mid nineteenth century, Munich's brewers responded with an everyday session lager and named the style 'Helles' (aka 'Hell'). Typically, the beers are malty with gentle bitterness and very easy to drink. A version called 'Hellesbock' denotes a stronger version of the style.

Drink this in a sunny beer garden and for a refreshing and easy drinking libation.

Glassware: lager

Good examples: Innstadt Neues Helles by Innstadt Brauerei (Passau, Germany); Hells Lager by Camden Town Brewery (London)

Serving temperature: 2–7 °C

Yeast: cool-fermenting

Typical ABV: 4–5%

What food? Calamari, chowder, corn on the cob, crab, dim sum, egg dishes such as omelettes and quiche, fish cakes, Indian (mild), lobster, shellfish, white fish.

Imperial Stout (aka Imperial Russian Stout)

See the entry below for 'Stout'.

India Pale Ale (IPA)

Characteristics: golden to amber in colour. Aromatic grapefruit, herbal, highly hopped, dry, medium to full body, refreshing, medium to high bitterness.

This beer was rebranded as 'India ale' about forty years after it had first been exported to the subcontinent in the mid eighteenth century. Originally the style was known as October beer – pale, highly hopped, high-alcohol and brewed in October to keep through the winter. Today this style should be a hop lover's nirvana – with aroma and bittering hops used liberally to create a brew for grown-ups, or people with cast-iron tongues. One of Britain's biggest-selling ales is Greene King IPA but really it is a malty bitter, not an India pale ale, and so when unsuspecting drinkers familiar with the Greene King brand try an authentic IPA they are in for a shock. American and British brewers have experimented by brewing black IPAs (with dark roasted malts) and 'Double' or 'Imperial' IPAs, which, as the former name suggests, means double the amount of hops – they are also high-alcohol, at 5–8% for IPA and 6–14% for Double or Imperial IPA.

Drink this for a journey into 'Hoplandia'. If you like bitterness and aroma, this is the beer for you.

Glassware: English pint, or dimpled barrel

Good examples: India Pale Ale by Meantime Brewing (London); Myrcenary by Odell Brewing Company (Fort Collins, Colorado, USA); Conqueror Black IPA by Windsor & Eton Brewery (Windsor, Berkshire)

Serving temperature: 11–13 °C

Yeast: warm-fermenting

Typical ABV: 5–14%

What food? Avocado, burgers, chilli con carne, creamy cheese, falafel, fish and chips, Indian (spicy), satay, grilled or smoked salmon, Thai, Vietnamese.

Kellerbier

Characteristics: amber in colour, cloudy in clarity. Caramel, toasty malt, light to medium body, medium hoppy bitterness.

This is a rare medieval German style of unfiltered and unpasteurised amber-coloured beer matured in wooden casks in underground vaults – hence the name 'Keller' (cellar). It resembles some British cask-conditioned ales but as it is made with cool-fermenting yeast it falls into the lager category.

Drink this if you like British amber cask-conditioned ales.

Glassware: lager or stein

Good examples: Griess Kellerbier by Brauerei Griess (Strullendorf-Geisfeld, Germany); Ayinger Kellerbier by Brauerei Aying (Aying, Germany)

Serving temperature: 6–10 °C

Yeast: cool-fermenting

Typical ABV: 4–7%

What food? Hummus, pizza, ploughman's, sausage and mash.

Kölsch

Characteristics: pale straw in colour. Perfumed light fruity aroma, dry malty taste, light to medium body, medium bitterness.

This style of easy-drinking ale originated in Cologne in Germany and was an attempt to entice nineteenth-century drinkers away from the increasingly popular Pilsners (which came from what we now know as the Czech Republic). According to European Union law, only brewers in the Cologne region are permitted to market this style as Kölsch but American brewers are not bound by the same legal rules so many US brewers make their versions of this beer. Despite this being ale, it should be drunk at a low temperature.

Drink this when in the mood for a light easy-drinking but flavoursome beer.

Glassware: Kölsch

Good examples: Mühlen Kölsch by Brauerei zur Malzmühle Schwartz (Cologne, Germany); Sion Kölsch by Kölner Verbund Brauereien (Cologne, Germany)

Serving temperature: 5–10 °C

Yeast: warm-fermenting

Typical ABV: 4–6%

What food? Calamari, cheese on toast, chowder, corn on the cob, dim sum, egg dishes such as omelettes and quiche, fish cakes, grilled white fish, Indian (mild), salads, shellfish.

Kriek (aka Cerise)

Characteristics: cherry pink in colour. Cherry, vanilla, tangy, sour-sweet, medium body, no bitterness.

Kriek means 'cherry' in Flemish and this Belgian style of beer does not conceal its fruity provenance. It often has an almond character in aroma and flavour derived from the fruit pips. The base beer is normally Lambic (see the entry for 'Lambic' for a description) with macerated cherries added during maturation. A skilful brewer will blend different-aged Lambics to create a spritzy tart beer with a hint of sweetness. Some brewers make cheaper versions with brown ale rather than Lambic and add fruit syrup – these tend to be sweeter and lack the necessary sourness to make it refreshing rather than sickly. Authentic Lambic Kriek is fermented with wild yeast and other microflora.

Drink this for a refreshing sour-sweet fruit burst and if you fancy a merry from a cherry.

Glassware: flute, snifter or tulip

Good examples: Alvinne Kriek van Mortagne by Picobrouwerij Alvinne (Moen, Belgium); 3 Fonteinen Kriekenlambik (Beersel, Belgium)

Serving temperature: 6–10 °C

Yeast: wild-fermenting

Typical ABV: 3.5–6%

What food? Ceviche, creamy cheese, Chinese (sweet and sour), chocolate puddings, coffee puddings, crème brûlée, melon, oysters, pâté.

Kristallweizen

See entry below for 'Weizen'.

Lambic

Characteristics: colour varies depending on blends. Cloudy in clarity. Sour fruit, dry, tart, medium body, no bitterness.

In most other styles sourness would be undesirable and a sign of stale beer. But this characteristic is what makes Lambics so extraordinary and quite unlike other beers. Some might say they resemble cider or dry white wine more than beer but they are beer – made from barley and wheat with aged hops used only for their preservative quality and not bitterness or aroma. In Belgium the distinctive mouth-puckeringly tart character of these beers derives from the fact they are fermented with wild yeast such as *Brettanomyces* and other microflora that live in the air around the brewery, or in the timbers of the structure itself, or in wooden casks in which the beer is matured for up to three years. They are a speciality of Belgium's Pajottenland region, although many US craft brewers have enthusiastically embraced this style. Of all beers in the world Lambics are possibly the most challenging and consequently brewers usually blend younger with mature beers to make them more mellow and drinkable, or they add fruit as in the case of Kriek and Frambozen. The beers are sour, dry, spritzy, earthy and complex.

Drink this if you fancy a surprise! It might remind you more of grapefruit juice, cider, or acidic white wine than beer. If you are wedded to malty caramel brews then this is not your beer, but try it to appreciate how diverse beer is.

Glassware: flute or tumbler

Good examples: Cantillon Bruocsella 1900 Grand Cru by Cantillon (Brussels, Belgium); De la Senne Crianza by Brasserie de la Senne (Brussels, Belgium)

Serving temperature: 10–13 °C

Yeast: warm-fermenting

Typical ABV: 3.5–7%

What food? Avocado, fish cakes, pâté, oily fish such as mackerel and salmon, shellfish.

Light ale

See the entry for 'Bitter'.

Maibock

See the entry for 'Bock'.

Märzen aka Oktoberfestbier

Characteristics: copper in colour. Rich, bready, toasted caramel malt, medium body, low to medium bitterness.

A German style traditionally brewed in March (*März*) so it matures in time for Oktoberfest. Before electronic refrigeration was invented, beer brewed in summer often went off, so sixteenth-century Bavarian ruler Duke Albrecht V decreed that brewing must cease between April and 29 September each year. Brewers had to make enough beer beforehand to last through the warm months and store (or lager) it in cool cellars or caves packed with ice. Any beer remaining when brewing resumed had to be consumed quickly so the barrels could be reused for the new brews. The tradition of drinking lots of beer at the end of September and the beginning of October was formalised in 1810 when Crown Prince Ludwig threw a gigantic party to celebrate his wedding and forty thousand citizens of Munich turned up. Today's Oktoberfest still takes place on the site of Ludwig's original grand beer bash.

Drink this to celebrate Oktoberfest and for a toasted, malty flavoursome brew.

Glassware: lager or stein

Good examples: Ayinger Oktober Fest-Märzen by Brauerei Aying (Aying, Germany); Augustinerbräu Kloster Mülln Märzen by Augustiner Bräu Kloster Mülln (Salzburg, Austria)

Serving temperature: 8–10 °C

Yeast: cool-fermenting

Typical ABV: 4–7%

What food? Charcuterie, cheese on toast, cheese dishes, pizza, potato dishes, pork dishes, roasted chicken duck, goose or turkey, sausages.

Mild

Characteristics: light amber to mahogany in colour. Malty, caramel, biscuit, chocolate, low bitterness.

Mild comes in two versions – light and dark – with a good malty base and usually a gentle hop character. The style has been brewed in England since at least as far back as the seventh century but is a misunderstood style of ale. People often assume 'mild' refers to the low bitterness of many milds, but historically the word actually referred to a young beer that was not matured. It normally had fewer hops because it did not need to age and was delivered to the pubs quickly enough after brewing that customers could drink the beer before it went sour. It was one of the beers that kept Britain's industrial workers refreshed and even now it has a cloth-cap image, its heartland of popularity being areas of current or former heavy industry – the west Midlands, and north-west England. In an era when highly hopped beers make most of the headlines amongst discerning beer drinkers in Britain and the USA, mild is out of fashion despite beers of this style winning Supreme Champion Beer of Britain four times since 2000 in the annual Great British Beer Festival. CAMRA ensures that the style is highlighted each May when brewers are encouraged to brew a mild because 'May is mild month'.

Drink this to keep the style alive and for an easy-drinking, malty, lightly hopped and refreshing session beer.

Glassware: English pint, or dimpled barrel

Good examples: Dark Ruby Mild by Sarah Hughes Brewery (Dudley, West Midlands); Black Cat by Moorhouse's Brewery (Burnley, Lancashire)

Serving temperature: 11–13 °C

Yeast: warm-fermenting

Typical ABV: 3–7%

What food? Lasagne, pizza, mushroom dishes, ploughman's, sausage and mash, shepherd's pie.

Münchener/Münchner

This means 'Munich-style' lager and can refer to Dunkels or Helles (see entries above).

Oktoberfest Märzen

See the entry for 'Märzen'.

Old ale

Characteristics: amber to mahogany in colour. Dried fruit, caramel malt, sherry-like, full body, medium bitterness.

An English style of beer, but don't be put off by the term 'old' – it denotes a smooth, well-matured rich fruity beer. Old ales have big flavours and body with high alcohol levels. In past centuries this style was sometimes known as 'stock ale', which meant it could be kept in stock and matured for long periods.

Drink this for a full-flavoured, full-bodied, strong, fruity, grown-up beer that is big on the malt.

Glassware: snifter

Good examples: Old Tom by Robinsons Brewery (Stockport, Greater Manchester); Prize Old Ale by George Gale (London)

Serving temperature: 11–13 °C

Yeast: warm-fermenting

Typical ABV: 6–10%

What food? Barbeque, full-flavoured English cheese, sausage and mash, game, stew, lasagne, mushroom dishes, roast Sunday lunch.

Oud bruin

Characteristics: dark ruby to copper brown in colour. Spicy, caramel, dried fruit and slightly sour, medium body, no bitterness.

A vinegary smell or taste is usually a bad sign in a beer but with this Belgian 'old brown' ale it is a characteristic of the style. The name comes from the tradition of aging the beer for months to years in oak barrels, where wild yeast and other microflora in the wood impart gentle sourness. Brewers quite often blend aged beers with younger ones for a smoother palate.

Drink this for a complex, fruity, sour beer.

Glassware: snifter or tulip

Good examples: Oud Bruin by Liefmans (Oudenaarde, Belgium); Petrus Oud Bruin by Bavik-De Brabandere (Harelbeke, Belgium)

Serving temperature: 10–13 °C

Yeast: warm-fermenting

Typical ABV: 4–8%

What food? Ceviche, Chinese (sweet and sour), grilled sardines, moules marinière, oysters, pâté, ploughman's, stew.

Pale ale

Characteristics: pale straw to amber in colour. Biscuit, sharp, floral, spicy, fruity, dry, medium body, high bitterness.

An English style that evolved in the seventeenth century when pale-coloured malts became available due to new malting techniques. The word 'pale' was relative to the dark beers that were prevalent at the time. Technically a bitter is a pale ale even though some of them are not all that pale. Nowadays beers marketed as pale ale do tend to be pale-coloured.

Drink this for a refreshing, sharp, aromatic and bitter drinking experience.

Glassware: English pint, or dimpled barrel

Good examples: Mary Jane by Ilkley Brewery (Ilkley, West Yorkshire); Festival Gold by Waen Brewery (Llanidloes, Powys, Wales)

Serving temperature: 10–13 °C

Yeast: warm-fermenting

Typical ABV: 3.5–5.5%

What food? Creamy cheese, falafel, fish and chips, Indian (spicy), quiche, satay, grilled or smoked salmon, Thai, Vietnamese.

Pilsner aka Pilsener lager

Characteristics: golden in colour. Herbal aroma, sharp, crisp, dry, light-bodied, spicy, firm bitterness.

In 1842 Pilsner Urquell first brewed a type of beer that would become the most popular style in the world. It originated in the Bohemian town of Pilsen (now in the Czech Republic), from where the term 'Pilsner' derives. The mineral content of the local water meant that beer brewed there was light-bodied, crisp and refreshing. The best Pilsners are usually brewed in the Czech Republic and Germany and should be sharp, well-hopped and zesty.

Unfortunately the style has been bowdlerised by so many brewers around the world that many people sneer at Pilsner as a bland characterless brew with little difference to fizzy water. The generic term 'lager' often refers to this style or versions of it.

Drink this for a crisp, refreshing, wakey-wakey, everyday beer.

Glassware: flute or Pilsner

Good examples: Budweiser Budvar Kroužkovaný Ležák by Budweiser Budvar České Budějovice (České Budějovice, Czech

Republic); Pilsner Urquell Kvasnicový by Plzensky Prazdroj (Plzeň, Czech Republic)

Serving temperature: 5–10 °C

Yeast: cool-fermenting

Typical ABV: 4–6%

What food? Falafel, fish and chips, grilled white fish, Indian (spicy), oily fish such as salmon, sardines, tuna and mackerel, seafood, Vietnamese.

Porter

Characteristics: mahogany in colour. Rich chocolate, coffee, caramel, nutty, savoury, roasted, dry, medium to full body, medium bitterness.

Named after the street and river porters of London who enthusiastically drank this dark beer, the style originated in London in the early eighteenth century and came to be known as the 'Entire Butt' before earning its more familiar moniker. The beer was a stronger, more hopped, matured version of the sweeter brown ale that was popular at the time. It was exported around the world including to Ireland where a Dublin brewer decided he would start brewing a local version of it. His name was Arthur Guinness.

Drink this for a rich coffee and chocolate full-bodied flavoursome brew.

Glassware: English pint, or chalice

Good examples: Powerhouse Porter by Sambrook's Brewery (London); Old Moor Porter by Acorn Brewery (Barnsley, Yorkshire)

Serving temperature: 8–13 °C

Yeast: warm-fermenting

Typical ABV: 4–7%

What food? Most desserts, in particular apple crumble and crème brûlée, anything chocolatey, barbecue, hearty food, shepherd's pie, steak, Stilton cheese.

Quadruple (Quad)

See the entries for 'Abbey' and 'Trappist' beers. The name refers to an alcohol level of typically 8–14% ABV.

Rauchbier

Characteristics: mahogany in colour. Smoky, malty toast, medium body, low bitterness.

How does a packet of Frazzles or smoky bacon crisps in beer form sound? So wrong it's right? *Rauch* is the German word for 'smoke' and this sixteenth-century Bavarian speciality derives its distinctive flavour because the malts are dried over a beechwood fire. At first taste some people are shocked but persevere to the third mouthful because by then the brain will be used to it. The beers are dark and come in Märzen, Bock and wheat versions – though all share the same assertively smoked character.

Drink this for an unexpected beer experience. If smoky flavour in a beer does not appeal just imagine it as a bacon sandwich in a glass – liquid breakfast.

Glassware: lager or stein

Good examples: Aecht Schlenkerla Rauchbier Märzen by Brauerei Heller (Bamberg, Germany); Spezial Rauchbier Weissbier by Brauerei Spezial (Bamberg, Germany)

Serving temperature: 8–13 °C

Yeast: warm or cool-fermenting, depending on the version

Typical ABV: 4–7%

What food? Anything smoked (e.g. ham, fish), barbeque, cheese dishes, Chinese food (especially mushroom or oyster sauce based dishes), Mexican food, mushrooms, sausages.

Red ale

Characteristics: tawny chestnut in colour. Malty biscuit, fruity, dry, medium body, medium bitterness.

This style earns its name from the malts used to brew it. More of the flavour comes from the malts than the hops so expect smooth caramel and toastiness.

Drink this if you like full-flavoured rich malty ales.

Glassware: English pint, or dimpled barrel

Good examples: Odd Ball by Offbeat Brewery (Crewe, Cheshire); Yakima Red by Meantime (London)

Serving temperature: 11–13 °C

Yeast: warm-fermenting

Typical ABV: 4–6%

What food? Barbeque, burgers, cheese dishes, classic pub grub – pies, sausage and mash, fish and chips, lasagne, macaroni cheese, ploughman's, sandwiches, shepherd's pie, steak, Sunday roast.

Roggenbier

Characteristics: copper in colour. Malty bread, slightly tart sour-sweet, spicy fruit, light to medium body, medium bitterness.

Roggen means 'rye' in German so that's what you get with this beer, a pocket full of rye mixed with barley. The style originated in Bavaria in the medieval era but production ceased when the Reinheitsgebot of 1516 (a German law that banned any other cereal in beer apart from barley) came into effect. It was revived in the 1980s but is not a widely brewed style of beer in its home country. If you find it, it is likely to be unfiltered and consequently cloudy. Several American craft brewers have revived the style but mostly on a special or seasonal brewing basis.

Drink this for a refreshing malty brew, to taste what rye does when combined with barley in beer, and to keep the style alive.

Glassware: lager

Good example: Bürgerbräu Wolnzacher Roggenbier by Bürgerbräu Wolnzach (Wolnzach, Germany); Roggenbier by Paulaner Bräuhaus (Munich, Germany)

Serving temperature: 8–13 °C

Yeast: warm-fermenting

Typical ABV: 5–7%

What food? Barbeque, cheese on toast, macaroni cheese, roast beef, roast chicken, roast pork, sausages.

Saison

Characteristics: rich golden colour. Spice, citrus fruit, dry, earthy, refreshing, medium body, medium bitterness.

Saison is the French for 'season' and the alternative name for this Belgian style is 'farmhouse ale'. Traditionally it was brewed in winter and stored until summer to refresh seasonal farm labourers as they toiled in the fields. They are dry, complex beers with a spiced fruit character.

Drink this if you are in the mood for a dry, complex, spicy brew.

Glassware: tulip

Good examples: Saison Dupont Vieille Provision by Brasserie Dupont (Tourpes-Leuze, Belgium); Saison D'Erpe-Mere Zymatore by KleinBrouwerij De Glazen Toren (Erpe-Mere, Belgium)

Serving temperature: 8–10 °C

Yeast: warm-fermenting

Typical ABV: 5–8%

What food? Charcuterie, Indian (spicy), falafel, fish and chips, Mexican, oily fish such as smoked salmon, seafood, satay, spicy duck, Thai, white fish.

Schwarzbier

Characteristics: dark brown in colour. Toasted malt, mild coffee, brown sugar, ripe fruit, dry, light to medium body, medium bitterness.

The name means 'black beer' in German but do not think of this as stout because these beers use cool-fermenting yeasts and so the body is relatively light but with depth of flavour.

Drink this if you like dark beers with a toasted malt character but light body.

Glassware: dimpled barrel, or lager

Good examples: Bayerischer Bahnhof Heizer Schwarzbier by Gasthaus & Gosebrauerei Bayerischer Bahnhof (Leipzig, Germany); Altstadthof Schwarzbier by Hausbrauerei Altstadthof (Nuremberg, Germany)

Serving temperature: 8–10 °C

Yeast: cool-fermenting

Typical ABV: 4–5.5%

What food? Barbeque, burgers, chocolate desserts, ham dishes, ice cream, kebabs, smoked dishes, Sunday roast.

Scotch ale

Characteristics: copper in colour. Caramel, spicy fruit, malty, medium body, low bitterness.

This is a nineteenth-century Scottish style of beer with full body, big malty fruity flavours and a warming character. Depending on the strength it is also known by the historic names of 60, 70, 80 or 90 shilling (often represented on pump clips with the symbol /-), which referred to the duty rates paid on the beer, with the latter nicknamed 'wee heavy'.

Drink this if you like malty, fruity flavoursome brews along the lines of an Extra Special Bitter.

Glassware: thistle or chalice

Good examples: Scotch Ale by Black Isle Brewery (Black Isle, near Inverness, Scotland); Ægir Lindisfarne Scotch Ale by Ægir Bryggeri (Flåm, Norway)

Serving temperature: 5–10 °C

Yeast: warm-fermenting

Typical ABV: 4–7%

What food? Barbeque, burgers, cheese dishes, lasagne, Forfar bridie, 'haggis, neeps and tatties', pies, ploughman's, shepherd's pie, sausage and mash, Sunday roast.

Smoked beer

See the entry for 'Rauchbier'.

Steam beer aka California common

Characteristics: amber in colour. Crisp, malty, hint of fruit, light to medium body, firm bitterness.

This is one of the very few styles of beer invented in the USA. The term 'steam beer' is a trademark now owned by Anchor Brewery in San Francisco, so other brewers of this style must call their version California Common. Anchor Brewery explains the origin of the name came in the nineteenth century from the steam that was produced when the hot brew was cooled quickly in shallow fermenting vessels. A strain of lager (cool-fermenting) yeast that ferments at higher-than-normal temperatures for that type of yeast gives this beer its character somewhere between lager and ale.

Drink this for a refreshing, pale, crisp beer with a good bitter hop character.

Glassware: lager

Good examples: Anchor Steam Beer by Anchor Brewing Company (San Francisco, California, USA); Russian River Beer Esteam by Russian River Brewing (Santa Rosa, California, USA)

Serving temperature: 3–8 °C

Yeast: cool-fermenting

Typical ABV: 4–6%

What food? Fish and chips, oily fish, pizza, seafood, spicy food.

Stout

Characteristics: mahogany to black in colour. Rich, roasted, charred, treacle, coffee, liquorice, medium to full body, firm bitterness.

Originally the name 'stout' referred to any strong English beer regardless of colour, so it was possible to have stout pale ales. The first reference to 'stout' in connection with beer was recorded in the 1630s.

When porter beers grew in popularity in the nineteenth century, stout became a term most associated with dark beers. Today there are several styles of dark stout but what they have in common is the colour – pitch black – and a roasted flavour. Oyster stouts sometimes, but not always, contain oysters. Oysters have such a subtle flavour that it is hard to notice them but traditionally they were eaten with stout or porter to wash them down. Milk stouts have a slight sweetness that comes from unfermentable sugars, usually lactose, hence the milk connection, added by the brewer. Oatmeal stouts have a smooth mouthfeel and a hint of sweetness from the addition of oats to the barley malts. Irish dry stouts tend to have an astringent mouthfeel that comes from roasted unmalted barley mixed in with malted barley. Imperial Russian stouts have a treacle-like consistency with a vinous characteristic and are the longest-aged, and of all stouts the biggest in body, flavour and alcohol level. Invented in London, the Russia connection comes from the popularity of these beers in the imperial court. Catherine the Great was said to be a great fan of this style.

Drink this for the love of dark rich coffee, roasted or even burnt flavours.

Glassware: English pint, or tulip

Good examples: Triple Chocoholic Stout by Saltaire Brewery (Saltaire, West Yorkshire); Oyster Stout by Porterhouse Brewing Company (Dublin, Ireland); O'Hara's Irish Stout by Carlow Brewing Company (Bagenalstown, Co. Carlow, Ireland); Alaskan Stout (Oatmeal) by Alaskan Brewing Company (Juneau, Alaska, USA); Imperial Russian Stout by Courage (Bedford, Bedfordshire)

Serving temperature: 8–16 °C

Yeast: warm-fermenting

Typical ABV: 4–12%

What food? Apple crumble, banana dishes, chocolate desserts, crème brûlée, ice cream, Mexican, shepherd's pie, strongly flavoured cheese such as Stilton, tiramisu.

Trappist

Characteristics: colour varies from light amber to mahogany. Spicy, caramel, tobacco, fruity, malty, phenolic, medium to high body, low bitterness.

Trappist is not a style *per se*, rather a collection of beers that share similar characteristics: candi sugar added to the brew, unpasteurised and bottle-conditioned. According to the International Trappist Association, to be labelled as a Trappist beer it must be brewed in a monastery by or supervised by monks. Currently only nine brands can claim to be an authentic Trappist beer. They are Achel, Chimay, La Trappe, Orval, Mont des Cats (not brewing in the monastery at present), Rochefort, Westvleteren, Westmalle and Stift Engelszell.

Orval is completely different to the other Trappist beers, being dry and earthy – these characteristics come from fermentation with wild *Brettanomyces* yeast in addition to cultured *Saccharomyces cerevisiae*.

Drink this if you like strong, full-flavoured, complex beers blessed by monks.

Glassware: chalice

Good examples: Rochefort Trappistes by Brasserie de Rochefort (Rochefort, Belgium); Westmalle Trappist by Brouwerij der Trappisten van Westmalle (Malle, Belgium)

Serving temperature: 8–13 °C

Yeast: warm-fermenting

Typical ABV: 5–12%

What food? Big flavoured beers suit big flavoured foods such as bacon dishes, spare ribs, charcuterie, roast duck or goose, game (including rabbit), goulash, mushroom dishes, cheese pasta dishes, pâté, roast lamb, salami, sausages, truffles, turkey, venison.

Tripel

See the entries for 'Abbey' and 'Trappist'. The Flemish word *tripel* (triple) refers to alcohol strength (typically 8–12% ABV).

Vienna lager

Characteristics: copper in colour. Toffee, bready, crisp, light to medium body, medium bitterness.

Despite originating in the eponymous city in Austria in the 1840s, most brewers of this type of beer today are in the USA and Mexico. Another name for this style is 'amber lager'.

Drink this for a crisp, refreshing, flavourful lager with a hint of caramel.

Glassware: lager

Good examples: Samuel Adams Boston Lager by Boston Beer Company (Boston, Massachusetts, USA); Brooklyn Lager by Brooklyn Brewery (Brooklyn, New York, USA)

Serving temperature: 5–8 °C

Yeast: cool-fermenting

Typical ABV: 3.5–6.5%

What food? Avocado, barbeque, burgers, fish and chips, Mexican, pasta with cheese or meat sauces, pies, pizza, roast chicken, satay, sausage and mash, steak.

Weissbier

See the entry for 'Weizen'.

Weizen

Characteristics: pale straw to mahogany in colour, cloudy in clarity. Aromatic, spicy, tart, full-bodied, low bitterness.

Weizen is the German word for 'wheat' and by law these beers, when brewed in Germany, must be at least 50 per cent wheat and the remainder barley. They are very distinctive beers due to the strain of yeast used to ferment them, which imparts banana and clove aromas. Weizen beers are cloudy due to wheat protein (which also accounts for the voluptuous pillowy head) and suspended yeast. This haze explains two other monikers for this style: Hefeweizen (*Hefe* is German for 'yeast') and Weiss (white) beer. All three names denote the same thing. If a beer is described as Kristallweizen it has been filtered of yeast and will be clear not cloudy, and the banana aroma will be subtle. Dunkelweizen is dark and has the characteristics described above but with a chocolatey character. Weizenbock is a dark, strong wheat beer with toasty caramel malt and dried fruit flavours.

Drink this when in the mood for tart, refreshing, full-bodied beer with low bitterness, or if you like the spicy fruit characteristics that wheat yeast imparts.

Glassware: weizen

Good examples: Schneider Weisse Unser Aventinus (a Weizenbock) by Weissbierbrauerei G. Schneider & Sohn (Kelheim, Germany); Weihenstephaner Hefeweissbier by Bayerische Staatsbrauerei Weihenstephan (Freising, Germany); Hefeweissbier Dunkel by Bayerische Staatsbrauerei Weihenstephan (Freising, Germany)

Serving temperature: 5–8 °C

Yeast: warm-fermenting

Typical ABV: 4.5–9%

What food? Weizen is one of the most versatile beers for food, including banana split, cheese on toast, Chinese, egg dishes (especially breakfast dishes, omelettes and quiche), fish cakes, hummus, grilled white fish, Indian (mild), seafood, smoked salmon, sushi, Thai.

Weizenbock

See the entry for 'Weizen'.

Wheat beer

See the entry for 'Weizen'.

White beer

See the entries for 'Weizen' and 'Witbier'.

Witbier

Characteristics: pale straw in colour, cloudy in clarity. Spicy, tart, apples, cloves, medium body, low bitterness.

Although at first sight and sip it might resemble a German Weizen, this crisp style of wheat beer is Belgian and has a distinct difference. That is the inclusion of coriander, orange peel and sometimes oats in the list of ingredients. Quite often a percentage of unmalted wheat is also added. The word '*wit*' is Flemish for white and this is due to the typical wheat-beer pale haze. In French these beers are known as *bières blanches*. A warm-fermenting special Belgian yeast accounts for the spicy aroma.

Drink this when in the mood for tart, refreshing beer with a spicy undertow and distinctive yeast that imparts clove and banana character.

Glassware: tumbler or weizen

Good examples: Hoegaarden by Brouwerij Hoegaarden (Hoegaarden, Belgium); St Bernardus Blanche by St Bernardus Brouwerij (Watou, Belgium)

Serving temperature: 5–7 °C

Yeast: warm-fermenting

Typical ABV: 4.5–9%

What food? Witbier is an exceedingly versatile beer for matching food, including cheese on toast, Chinese, egg dishes (especially breakfast, omelettes and quiche), fish cakes, hummus, grilled white fish, Indian (mild), seafood, smoked salmon, sushi, Thai.

SAVE A LIFE – DRINK BEER

It is well known that one reason why, throughout history, humans consumed beer was to avoid drinking polluted water. Even children drank beer, albeit a low-alcohol (approximately 2% ABV) version known in English as 'small beer'. That term is now used to describe something almost worthless but originally it was the libation that prevented people from being poisoned by water. In Britain until pure, safe water from the mains was readily available in the early part of the twentieth century, children would have continued to drink small beer.

Proof that beer can be a lifesaver was a cholera outbreak in London's Soho district in 1854. Cholera, fairly common in cities, had been assumed to be caused by miasma (bad air) but physician Dr John Snow suspected it was a waterborne disease. He had observed that men who worked in a brewery and drank beer rather than local water did not contract cholera when other people in the area did. Dr Snow mapped the epidemic and pinpointed a public water pump that he concluded was spreading the pathogen. His suspicion was correct – human waste had leaked into the water supply. On his instruction the pump was disabled and no new cases of cholera were reported. Today there is an eponymous pub near the site of his research on Broadwick Street.

WHAT IS 'CRAFT BEER'?

Craft beer is hard to define, because it has much to do with the attitude of the brewer and the drinker's experience in the boozer. Pubs that sell craft beer tend to have a modern twist even if the interior looks traditional, with a younger demographic, more women, and fewer old-fashioned 'anoraks' and 'tickers' (the trainspotters of beer, who make lists of the brews they have sampled and carry the log of their drinking life everywhere they go, comparing notes with other tickers).

Craft beer is often used to describe small independent breweries that make bold, innovative, flavourful beers. They are often experimental and less beholden to tradition than their larger and more established counterparts. The beers they make are less 'products' and more a passion to share with other beerios. With craft breweries it is the brewer – not the 'suits' in the marketing department – who decides on the beers and the recipes.

However, the term 'craft beer' is currently so fashionable that it is increasingly being hijacked by some brewers of rather ordinary beers in an attempt to make their brands stand out in a crowded market. The term has also largely replaced 'microbrewery', and in that context it does not say anything about the quality of the beer, but rather is related to size and usually refers to new brewing businesses.

The evolution of craft beer started with USA-based home brewers in the 1970s who, unable to buy decent beer, were inspired to make it themselves. Two of them, Ken Grossman and Doug Odell, went on to establish breweries – Sierra Nevada Brewing Co and Odell Brewing Co respectively – both of which now make world-class beers. They had a weapon in a number of US hop varietals that gave the beers spectacular aroma and flavour, and they were not afraid to use them! Compare Sierra Nevada Pale Ale with one of the mainstream and ubiquitous major American beer brands and the contrast could not be more apparent. The former is lovingly handcrafted and inspires rhapsody in its drinkers, the latter is purposely bland in order to appeal to the widest market possible and is made in industrial quantities with the bottom line as the priority.

One of the first British craft breweries to eschew the traditional cask-conditioned ale model was Meantime Brewing Company in London. Founded in the 1990s, it is now one of the capital's leading breweries. The brewer Alastair Hook, who reveres good beer whether cask or keg, began a revolution with a range of excellent beers such as London Pale Ale, Yakima Red and London Stout, none of which is served from a cask. Now there are countless such breweries in Britain, including Thornbridge

Brewery in Derbyshire, with their peerless Jaipur IPA, and Ilkley Brewery in West Yorkshire, with too many good beers to list, that could be described as craft brewers. They have brought an excitement to brewing and customer choice that is irresistible.

But this revolution in British brewing has led to a schism amongst the members of CAMRA, which was founded in 1971 by a small group of beer lovers who were disenchanted with the preponderance of insipid, poor-quality, fizzy, pasteurised beers that dominated the market at the time. Going for a pint then was rarely a memorable drinking experience the way it is now. It was time to fight back and, from a tiny core, CAMRA became one of the most effective consumer-campaigning organisations in Britain. Their approximately 150,000 members have such passion and zeal for cask-conditioned real ale that they have succeeded in creating a huge demand for Britain's national drink served in this most natural of ways. Without CAMRA, Britain's current brewing renaissance would not be so dynamic, for it proved there was a great thirst for natural, unpasteurised beer made by hand by your local brewer. They made it possible for British brewing to enter the current golden age, and also laid the foundations for craft beer.

And that is a problem to some CAMRA members. Craft beer does not necessarily mean 'real ale'. Some craft brewers only sell their beers in the pasteurised keg format. But these are not the tasteless beers of the 1970s that inspired the birth of CAMRA. Some members question why they spent years campaigning for real ale only for kegged beer to sneak in on the back of their efforts. However, other members of CAMRA (author included) support and enthusiastically consume flavoursome high-quality beer no matter what format it is served in.

Long live good beer – cask or keg!

In the Mood – What To Drink?

Beer describes a drink made from fermented cereal sugar and wine is a drink made from fermented fruit juice. But both are so diverse that to make an educated choice means knowing more about the ingredients. A wine drinker considers the grape: 'I'd like something dry and flinty so I'll go for a glass of Chablis', or more likely they peruse the extensive tasting notes on the wine list. Unfortunately few pubs provide such useful information about the beer they serve and members of staff do not always have the knowledge, either because they have not been trained in beer styles, or the brewery has not provided a full description of their beers. Bottled beer labels are often vague about the contents.

So when faced with a row of handpumps and taps in a pub, or a wall of bottles in a shop, how does one know what to choose? Some pubs are generous and let customers 'try before they buy', so the staff will pour a sample to help the customer decide. But in the absence of that service it's guesswork, or at least being restricted to the option of asking: 'Is it pale, amber, or dark?' Which is as informative as asking with wine: 'Is it red or white?'

When trying to decide what I want to drink, I imagine the taste of the beer to see what mood I am in. Is it malt, hops, fruit or spice? Is it light, medium or full body? Low-alcohol or high-alcohol? I also consider other factors. If I have cycled like a demon to the pub and am feeling thirsty then an imperial stout is unlikely to quench it, whereas hops will hit the spot. But if it is chilly outside and I am cosy by the fire then I would go for a big fruity abbey beer.

For a suggestion of which beers to choose depending on the mood your taste buds are in, look at the characteristics below and the styles that match them. Note that some beer styles fall into several categories.

Aromatic: abbey, Belgian strong dark ale, Belgian strong pale ale, India pale ale, pale ale, Weizen, witbier.

Bittersweet: barley wine, old ale.

Bready: blonde ale, Brut des Flandres, Dortmunder lager, Helles, Roggenbier, Vienna lager.

Caramel: abbey, Belgian strong dark ale, bière de garde, bitter, Bock, Doppelbock, Burton ale, English strong ale, Kellerbier, Märzen, mild, old ale, oud bruin, porter, Scotch ale, Trappist.

Chocolate: Dunkel, dark mild, porter, stout, imperial Russian stout.

Coffee: brown ale, porter, Schwarzbier, stout, imperial Russian stout.

Citrus: Berliner Weissbier, bitter, India pale ale, pale ale, saison, Weizen, witbier.

Complex: abbey, barley wine, Doppelbock, ESB, gueuze, imperial Russian stout, old ale, oud bruin, saison, Trappist.

Crisp: blonde ale, Brut des Flandres, Pilsner, steam beer, Vienna lager.

Dried fruit: abbey, Altbier, barley wine, Belgian strong dark ale, old ale, Trappist.

Dry/mineral: bitter, golden ale, India pale ale, gueuze, Kölsch, Lambic, pale ale, Pilsner, porter, red ale, saison, Schwarzbier, stout.

Easy-drinking: blonde ale, dinner ale, golden ale.

Earthy: bière de garde, saison.

Floral: bitter, Bock, Doppelbock, Brut des Flandres, golden ale, pale ale.

Full-bodied: abbey, barley wine, Burton ale, ESB, old ale, Weizen, imperial Russian stout, Trappist.

Fruity: bière de garde, blonde ale, Bock, Doppelbock, Brut des Flandres, Burton ale, English strong ale, ESB, Flanders red ale, Frambozen, golden ale, gueuze, Kriek, Lambic, oud bruin, pale ale, red ale, Trappist, witbier.

Herbal: Helles, India pale ale, Pilsner.

High-alcohol: abbey, barley wine, imperial Russian stout, old ale, Trappist.

High bitterness: bitter, India pale ale, pale ale, stout, imperial Russian stout.

Hoppy: bitter, Burton ale, India pale ale, pale ale.

Light-bodied: blonde ale, Brut des Flandres, dinner ale, Pilsner, Vienna lager.

Low bitterness: abbey, Belgian strong dark ale, Berliner Weissbier, brown ale, Brut des Flandres, dinner ale, Dunkel, Frambozen, Gose, gueuze, Kriek, Lambic, mild, oud bruin, Rauchbier, Scotch ale, Trappist, Weizen, witbier.

Malty/biscuit: Altbier, barley wine, Belgian strong dark ale, Belgian strong pale ale, bière de garde, blonde ale, Bock, Doppelbock, Burton ale, Dunkel, English strong ale, ESB, golden ale, Kölsch, Märzen, mild, pale ale, Rauchbier, red ale, Roggenbier, Schwarzbier, Scotch ale, Trappist.

Medium bitterness: Altbier, Belgian strong pale ale, bière de garde, blonde ale, Bock, Doppelbock, Dortmunder lager, English strong ale, golden ale, Kellerbier, Kölsch, Märzen, old ale, oud bruin, Pilsner, porter, red ale, Roggenbier, saison, Schwarzbier, steam beer, Vienna lager.

Nutty: Altbier, brown ale, Brut des Flandres, Doppelbock, Dunkel, mild, porter, Trappist.

Refreshing: Berliner Weissbier, gueuze, Helles, India pale ale, Kölsch, Lambic, Pilsner.

Roasted: porter, imperial Russian stout, stout.

Savoury: porter, imperial Russian stout, stout, strong ale.

Smoke: porter, Rauchbier.

Sour-sweet: Flanders red ale, Frambozen, Kriek, oud bruin, Roggenbier.

Spicy: abbey, Belgian strong dark ale, Belgian strong pale ale, bière de garde, oud bruin, India pale ale, pale ale, Roggenbier, saison, Trappist, Weizen, witbier.

Sweet: Doppelbock, brown ale, faro.

Tart: Berliner Weissbier, Gose, gueuze, Lambic, Roggenbier, Weizen.

Toasty: abbey, Altbier, barley wine, Belgian strong dark ale, bière de garde, ESB, Kellerbier, Märzen, Schwarzbier, Trappist.

Toffee: abbey, brown ale, Doppelbock, Dunkel, mild, porter, Trappist, Vienna lager.

Treacle: imperial Russian stout, Trappist.

Beer Hall of Fame

These are my beer heroes – some of them brewers, some breweries – and the brews that make them my pin-ups.

Dougal Sharpe

The genius behind Innis & Gunn, one of the most singular beer brands available. For anyone who has never tasted beers from this range, rush to the supermarket or call a beer retailer that will do an emergency next-day delivery, making sure you have some treacle tart in the house too to match with them. Innis & Gunn beers are aged in oak to give them rich vanilla, toffee, marmalade and whisky characters, which match perfectly with desserts such as crème brûlée, brandy snaps and profiteroles. But the beers also go with smoked fish, mildly spiced curry and roast lamb. Dougal can claim another accolade – he redeveloped the recipe for Deuchars IPA by Caledonian Brewery which went on to win many awards, including Supreme Champion Beer of Britain at the Great British Beer Festival in 2002.

Flying Dog (Maryland, USA)

Flying Dog is a beerio's best friend. This brewery is no poodle, though; it's a mastiff with some huge beers. Like some other American craft brewers, Flying Dog brews Old-World-style beers but with a New World spin. Some of their brews are one-offs or seasonals, but one regular brand worth trying is Snake Dog IPA with succulent citrus hops, a satisfyingly big body, and a long dry finish. Oh, and it is 7.1% ABV so you'll be smiling pretty soon after cracking it open.

Fuller's (London)

Among the range from London's oldest brewer there is a beer for everyone. For sheer variety can anyone beat Fuller's? From the light, crisp, easy-drinking Discovery Blonde Beer, through to London Porter or London Black Cab Stout and the peerless Vintage Ale, every taste and mood is covered. And they also make the classic English pint of bitter, London Pride.

Garrett Oliver

Brewmaster of Brooklyn Brewery in New York, Garrett is a great advocate for beer and food matching and author of the most definitive book on the subject, *The Brewmaster's Table*. His Black Chocolate Stout matched with Colston Bassett Stilton cheese is sublime. To hear Garrett speak about beer is like listening to a poet reciting love sonnets.

Ilkley Brewery

Three words to describe Yorkshire's Ilkley Brewery: open-minded, innovative and fun. They brew a diverse selection including the classic session beer Mary Jane, and also Ilkley Black mild, Lotus IPA, and Wit Marie (a wheat beer). A passion for experimentation is realised through their 'Origins' range in which they collaborate with beer writers and sommeliers (author included). So far this has led to such amazing potions as 'The Green Goddess', brewed with fresh hops, orange peel, Szechuan peppercorns and nigella seeds, and fermented with Belgian yeast; and 'The Norseman' – a spruce beer containing fir buds and pine needles foraged from Ilkley Moor.

Meantime Brewing Company (London)

Based in Greenwich of course, Meantime prove that kegged (pasteurised) beer can be exciting and full of flavour. London Pale Ale, London Lager, London Stout and India Pale Ale are favourites. About four years ago they brewed a one-off saison so delicious that I still dream about it.

Mikkeller (Denmark)

Founded by two Danish home brewers Mikkel Borg Bjergsø and Kristian Klarup Keller, Mikkeller is known as a 'gypsy' brewer: they do not have their own brewery but are cuckoos who travel the word, landing in the nests of other brewers in Denmark, Belgium, Britain, Norway and the USA to create some spectacular brews that ignore all the established rules. So far they have produced more than six hundred different beers – usually brewed only once – including Funky E-Star Sauternes Wine Barrel Aged (Belgian pale ale); George! Calvados Barrel Aged (imperial Russian stout); and Texas Ranger (Chipotle Porter) Framboise Edition (a hybrid smoky raspberry porter). Trying a new Mikkeller beer is always a special occasion and a workout for the taste buds.

Sara Barton

British Brewer of the Year 2012–2013, as voted by the British Guild of Beer Writers, Sara Barton runs Brewster's Brewery in Grantham and brews one of my desert island beers, Brewster's Pale Ale. She is the originator of Project Venus, an alliance of female British and Irish brewers who gather every three months to brew a new beer. Another reason for her award was because she is so willing to share the passion for her craft by inviting a number of beer lovers to realise their dreams of creating their very own recipe and then brewing it with her for sale in pubs. With 'Hophead' and 'Marquis', your session beers are sorted but if you fancy a change, then Brewster's constantly come up with new beers in their Wicked Women and Whimsicale ranges – some one-offs, others returning brews. Beautifully balanced beers.

Sierra Nevada

Five years ago I tried this California brewer's Torpedo IPA, and I can still remember the extraordinary tangerine aroma and the intensely flavourful bitterness. I loved it. Home brewer Ken Grossman opened Sierra Nevada brewery in 1980 to brew the types of hop-tastic beers he wanted to drink but could not buy commercially in the USA. Those bold aromas, flavours and high bitterness obtained from American hop varieties and pioneered by Sierra Nevada precipitated the second American Revolution, and British brewers and beer drinkers have embraced the innovation with gusto.

Sophie de Ronde

Head brewer at Brentwood Brewing Company in Essex and creator of a number of fine brews including Chockwork Orange (a rich porter brewed with oranges) and the singular After 8 (imperial Russian stout brewed with cocoa nibs and mint), Sophie also devised the recipe for the best low-alcohol beer I have ever tasted: BBC 2, an IPA in a bitter's clothing, is a mere 2.5% ABV but is so packed full of flavour one would never know. It takes real skill to brew a low-alcohol beer that not only has flavour but has body too. BBC 2 is the ultimate session beer and a gift for drivers who fancy a pint and want to stay within the legal limit.

Marston's Beer Company

Marston's had the genius idea of demonstrating to drinkers just what the hop does to beer. In the Single Hop Beer programme they use the same base of water, malt and yeast, then dramatically change the beer by adding a different single hop into each brew. The result is a spectacular showcase of the aroma and flavour of specific varietals from around the world, including Wakatu and Pacific Gem from New Zealand, Amarillo and El Dorado from the USA, and from England, Endeavour and the classic noble hop East Kent Goldings.

Nøgne Ø (Grimstad, Norway)

David to the Goliath of pale pasteurised lager that makes up 98 per cent of Norway's beer market, Nøgne Ø has laid down the gauntlet by brewing complex, full-bodied, high-alcohol brews. Most of them pay homage to British and Belgian styles, for instance brown ale, India pale ale, and saison. Be prepared for big, flavoursome beers.

Schneider & Sohn (Kelheim, Germany)

Worship the wheat! This German brewer specialises in Weisse beers and what a diverse range they have. For a classic wheat beer try Schneider Weisse Unser Original, and if that hits the spot work through the different versions such as Schneider Weisse Unser Aventinus, with a toffee character, and Schneider Weisse Mein Nelson Sauvin, made with the superstar Nelson Sauvin hop from New Zealand that imparts a lush tropical fruit aroma and flavour.

In the absence of date and walnut cake doused with maple syrup, the Aventinus Eisbock will suffice. A glass full of dried fruit, plums and toasted caramel with a smooth, rich body will bring glee to sweet-toothed beer lovers. Intense, complex, warming and strong (12% ABV) it is diabolically delicious.

The Wild Beer Co (Evercreech, Somerset)

The clue is in the name: what makes this brewery different is that they brew with strains of wild yeast rather than cultured *Saccharomyces cerevisiae*. Some of the beers are also aged in oak barrels. All their beers are complex and funky and show off the marvellous unpredictability of wild yeast. Modus Operandi (an old ale aged in oak barrels) and Epic Saison are two beers to try.

Thornbridge Brewery (Bakewell, Derbyshire)

Celebrated for their brilliant Jaipur IPA (which has won over two hundred industry and consumer awards) and Kipling South Pacific Pale Ale, all Thornbridge's brews are memorable. Halcyon Imperial IPA and Saint Petersburg Imperial Russian Stout are excellent examples of their style. Thornbridge also brew lager styles, including Kill Your Darlings (Vienna lager). Try them all!

Williams Brothers Brewing Company

This Scottish brewery is on my Valentine's card list not only for the superb Profanity Stout, but because of a range of beers that celebrate thousands of years of Scottish brewing heritage. For a taste of history try Fraoch, made with heather flowers, a style that has been brewed in Scotland for over four thousand years. Williams Brothers is the only brewery in the world still regularly brewing this type of beer. Other ancient brews in the range are Grozet, brewed with gooseberries; Ebulum, which includes elderberries in the brew; Kelpie, containing seaweed; and Alba, made with Scots pine. The latter is heavenly with panna cotta or cheesecake.

Looking Good – What Glassware?

Well, hello – don't you look gorgeous! Or so I often think about my beer, especially when it is served in my favourite tulip-style glass. We use all our senses when we drink, starting with sight, so presentation is important. Luckily, beer is served in a glass nowadays and we can see what we are about to sip – unlike our ancestors who were restricted to hollow animal horns, or to wooden, earthenware, pewter or leather tankards or mugs.

The shape and design of the glass can enhance the beer and even direct it to certain parts of the tongue so that specific characteristics are highlighted. For instance, beer sipped from a tall glass that is tapered at the rim will flow to the middle and back of the tongue, emphasising sharp and bitter flavours, and this shape will also concentrate aromas.

Although the glass police will not come and arrest you for using the vessel of your choice regardless of style, these suggestions of glassware might just make your drink even more enjoyable.

Chalice

If this model is reminiscent of something from the church altar, there's a reason – this style is also known as a Trappist glass, after the order of monks celebrated for their brewing prowess. These glasses are wide-rimmed bowls on a long stem. The design allows a big foamy head and complex aromas to develop, and encourages sipping, which means that the beer hits the front of the tongue where sweet and fruit flavours register. As well as presenting the beer in an elegant way, the shape also inspires a reverential attitude. All together now: 'For what we are about to drink, may Ninkasi make us truly thankful.'

Try a chalice with these beer styles:

Abbey (dubbel, tripel, quadrupel)
Burton ale
English strong ale
Extra special bitter (ESB)
Porter
Scotch ale
Trappist

Dimpled barrel

This is a thick dimpled mug with a handle. The mouth is larger than the base and this releases the aroma. These glasses are so solid that repeated lifting builds up the arm muscles.

Try a dimpled barrel with these styles:

Bitter
Pale ale
Brown ale
Dunkel
Golden ale
Gose
India pale ale (IPA)
Mild

Red ale
Schwarzbier

English pint

This is the classic glassware for beer served in British pubs. There are two versions: one is straight-sided, the other has a bulge in the top third and is often called a nonic (the design supposedly prevents it from being easily chipped, or nicked, hence the ironic nickname 'no nick'). Both have a wider mouth than base to release the aroma and the beer is sloshed onto the tongue so it makes contact with all the taste buds.

Try an English pint glass with these styles:

Bitter
Pale ale
Brown ale
Golden ale
India pale ale (IPA)
Mild
Red ale
Stout

Flute

A tall, narrow, delicate, elegant glass on a long stem. Most commonly used for Champagne, they are perfect for lighter, sparkling beers. The tapered rim pours the liquid towards the back of the tongue, enhancing effervescence and acidity.

Try a flute with these styles:

Brut des Flandres
Frambozen
Kriek
Lambic
Pilsner

Footed Pilsner

Tall and tapered like an inverted isosceles triangle, narrower at the bottom than the top, this shows off the colour and carbonation of the beer and, as the vessel's mouth is not too wide, it maintains a beer head. It has a short stem and foot.

Try a footed Pilsner with these styles:

Helles
Pilsner

Lager

A basic style of glass that holds approximately two-thirds of a pint of beer. They have gradual sloping sides and are wider at the mouth than at the base so this preserves the foam head.

Try a lager glass with these styles:

Dortmunder lager
Helles
Kellerbier
Märzen
Oktoberfest
Rauchbier
Schwarzbier

Steam beer
Vienna lager

Snifter

Due to its shape, bulbous and narrowing to the top, this style is sometimes called a balloon. They sit on a stem and a foot and turn the drinking of beer into an elegant ritual. The shape makes it easy to swirl the beer to release the aromas.

Try a snifter with these styles:

Barley wine
Bière de garde
Old ale
Oud bruin
Dinner ale
Flanders red ale
Frambozen
Kriek

Stein

Intricately decorated ceramic, earthenware or stoneware Bavarian beer jugs, these do little to enhance the beer but look great! Some steins have lids so aroma can waft out each time it is opened (and the lid prevents fag ash falling in…). There is also a glass version, but those are basic barrels with a handle that hold a litre of beer.

Try a stein with these styles:

Bock
Dunkel

Gose
Kellerbier
Märzen
Oktoberfest
Rauchbier

Tulip

Possibly the most perfectly shaped beer glass ever designed – it has a bulbous bottom on a stem and foot. The flared mouth retains a foamy head, and the beer is easy to swirl so the aromas are released. But more than anything, it makes beer look lip-smackingly lovely.

Try a tulip with these styles:

Belgian pale ale
Belgian strong ale
Bière de garde
English strong ale
Flanders red
Frambozen
Kriek
Imperial Russian stout
Oud bruin
Saison
Stout

Tumbler

These squat glasses are functional rather than graceful, with gently sloping straight sides and a wide mouth that promotes a sip rather than a glug. Sipping the beer, as with the chalice, means that it hits the front of the tongue first so any sweetness in the beer will register there.

Try a tumbler with these styles:

Frambozen
Kriek
Lambic
Witbier

Weizen

Tall, slender and flared at the top – ideal for accentuating the cloudy appearance of a wheat beer and for a voluptuous head formation.

Try a weizen with these styles:

Berliner Weisse
Bock
Weizen
Witbier

Wine glass

Wine glasses are on long stems and come in a variety of forms, from bowls to tulip-shaped. An ideal wine glass for beer is one with a tapered mouth that releases aromas. Although a wine glass is not a legal measure for draught beer served in a pub in Britain, there is no rule against using them for bottled beer – especially at a dinner table.

Any style of beer is good from a wine glass.

FANCY GOING OUT FOR A POTTLE?

In the history of beer, drinking out of glassware is a recent innovation. The Industrial Revolution and a decrease in glass tax spurred mass production; suddenly people could see the colour and clarity of what they were drinking, and this was a novelty.

But back in the early days of beer, a plethora of vessels were used to serve it in. Shells were amongst the earliest. Vikings and Celts are said to have drunk ale, mead and cider from their enemies' skulls. But in the absence of a real cranium a wooden bowl called a scole, resembling the top half of a human pate, would suffice. Hollow animal horns were often polished and trimmed with decoration, then attached to a leather thong to be carried over the shoulder. Wooden bowls were carved and smoothed – some were similar to buckets and called pottles; others were more elegant, shallow dishes on a broad foot and were known as mazers. Anglo-Saxons used 'tumblers' – oval-shaped vessels that would not balance so they had to be held, or the contents drained quickly. Most people had an ornamental drinking vessel for personal use. Viking and Saxon warriors were buried with theirs so they were prepared for the afterlife, where the drink never runs out.

Leather, wooden and pewter tankards made an appearance in the medieval era. In Britain, leather vessels were known as black jacks – they resembled riding boots (known as jacks) and that is where the term 'fill your boots' derives. An extra-large version of a black jack was known as a bombard because it looked like the mouth of a cannon of the same name. Toby jugs (pottery tankards) decorated to resemble old men wearing tricorn hats became fashionable in the eighteenth century. Nowadays weights and measures dictate the containers we drink from in a pub, so no chance of asking for a pint in a piggin – a small leather pitcher (the name is a diminutive of pigskin) – although some traditional real ale drinkers carry their own pint-sized pewter tankard with them. Perhaps they will ask to be buried with it too – after all, in heaven the beer is always fresh and there is never a queue at the bar.

A Little of What You Fancy Does You Good

Beer, if drank with moderation, softens the temper,
cheers the spirit and promotes health.

American Founding Father, Thomas Jefferson

Of all alcoholic drinks, beer has more health, nutritional and social benefits than any other.

Consumed moderately, beer has proven health benefits. Moderate consumption of low to medium-alcohol beer (4% ABV) is ten pints a week for men, eight pints a week for women, to be consumed throughout the week (with days off for the liver to have a rest but not, alas, to be saved up for a weekend binge). Dozens of independent medical experiments have concluded that the beer drinkers in their studies were happier and healthier than those who did not drink beer or drank too much. These positive facts about beer are not widely reported because problems caused by alcohol abuse take precedence in the media and there is a reluctance to be seen to be celebrating the drinking of alcohol.

In some British hospitals until at least the mid 1970s, trolleys containing bottles of beer were trundled around the wards, and patients, regardless of whether they were in for an ingrown toenail or cancer, were offered a drink. It was good for morale, but more than anything it was a motivation to get better, leave hospital and go to the pub – after all, it was only a small bottle of beer.

The Ancient Egyptians did not just drink beer for pleasure but also used it as medicine too, for ailments including gum disease, as dressing for wounds, and externally as a poultice to treat piles.

Today, one of the world's leading authorities on beer, Professor Charles Bamforth, is the author of the definitive work on the positive effects of drinking it. The science behind the health claims for beer is to be found in his book *Beer: Health and Nutrition.*

But before telling you the good news about beer to print on a T-shirt, or on a placard to carry round at all times so that naysayers can be enlightened, let us first dispel one particular and persistent myth about beer.

The belly

In every language a big stomach is known as a 'beer belly' or 'beer gut'. Some people who do not drink beer have a belly, yet it is still known as a beer belly. How can that be? It should be called a 'burger belly' because weight gain is caused by a person taking in more calories than they expend – it is lifestyle and not exercising enough that puts on the weight. Measure for measure beer has fewer calories than any other alcoholic drink. Here is a comparison of beer with other popular pub drinks and snacks:

Pint (568 ml) of 4% ABV beer = 190 calories

Medium-sized glass of white wine (175 ml) = 131 calories

Single gin and tonic (with a small bottle of tonic totals 150 ml) = 120 calories

Bottle of alcopop (275 ml) = range is 150–230 calories

Pint (568 ml) of orange juice = 256 calories

Pint (568 ml) of soft drink such as cola = 272 calories

Small packet of crisps = 183 calories

100 g packet of peanuts = 601 calories

And don't forget the doner kebab on the way home from the pub = 800–1000 calories (depending on size)

Beer contains no fat or cholesterol, and is low in carbohydrates and sugars. But some people feel bloated after drinking beer because carbon dioxide in beer warms in the stomach and swells. That is temporary and will soon go away. The answer is to drink lower-carbonated beer or ideally real ale.

So let us push the belly to one side and consider the health benefits of beer:

Antioxidants
Antioxidants are substances that help to protect the body against the effects of free radicals – molecules that can damage cells, and may trigger heart, cancer and other diseases. Both barley and hops contain antioxidants and consequently beer is rich in them.

The protection of ethanol (alcohol)
In small doses it can protect the body against a number of health problems, including the risk of coronary heart disease, by raising the amount of 'good' cholesterol (high-density lipoprotein), thereby

lowering the risk of arteriosclerosis (hardening of the arteries), type 2 diabetes, gallstones and Parkinson's disease.

The many benefits of hops

Hops are a rich source of the micronutrient phytoestrogen. Consumption of phytoestrogen is connected with a decreased incidence of breast cancer in humans. Supplements containing phytoestrogen are used as a natural hormone replacement therapy for post-menopausal women.

Hops can help to prevent calcium leaching from the bones, which is a reason why they found in medical studies that beer drinkers were less likely to suffer from calcium oxalate kidney stones and osteoporosis. Silicon in beer also helps to prevent the latter problem so beer drinkers have a double whammy in fighting that bone condition.

Medical research suggests that a group of antioxidants known as flavonoids present in hops may prevent the development of cardiovascular disease, obesity, diabetes and certain cancers.

Hops are also antibacterial and can prevent the growth of food-poisoning pathogens, such as *Clostridium difficile*, and heliobacteria, which are believed to cause stomach cancer, duodenal and gastric ulcers.

The properties of hops are also useful for purifying the blood, to stimulate a sluggish liver, and to treat a variety of ailments including insomnia, migraine, indigestion, intestinal cramps, earache, travel sickness, irritability and tension.

Nutritional benefits

Beer contains carbohydrates, proteins, minerals, vitamins, soluble fibre and amino acids. Also, as fermentation increases the nutritional value of food and drink, the malted cereal in beer is much more nutritious than it would be as breakfast cereal. B vitamins are particularly abundant in beer, as are potassium and silicon, and all three have specific benefits.

B vitamins: The B-vitamin complex is essential for the proper functioning of almost every process in the body, including the central nervous system, energy production, digestion, and the growth of healthy hair, skin and nails.

Potassium: Healthy bodies need potassium. A deficiency can lead to strokes, low blood sugar, muscle disorders, impaired brain function, abnormal blood pressure, heart disease, kidney disorders and stress.

Silicon: Silicon is not produced naturally by the body, but the body needs it nonetheless. Beer is one of the richest sources of silicon available to us (it exists in the husks of barley), which is good news as this essential mineral prevents our bodies from falling apart because of its involvement in the production of collagen – the protein in tendons, blood vessel walls, skin, nails and hair. It also maintains healthy joints and bone density, and that is the reason why the beer drinkers in medical studies were found less likely to suffer from osteoporosis than the non-drinkers. A daily intake of silicon of 25–30 mg is considered ideal and one pint of beer contains around 16 mg of it. Silicon can also help to block the brain's absorption of aluminium, a toxic metal believed to play a role in the onset of Alzheimer's disease and dementia. Therefore, another marvellous benefit of this mineral is its anti-aging properties. Drink beer and stay young!

Watery goodness

Beer is a way of consuming water, though much more fun than a few glasses of H_2O! But beware: the paradox is that some beer drinkers become dehydrated, because beer increases the urge to urinate. All that water, plus the fact that hops are diuretic means that water going in via beer goes out again very quickly. Think of beer as a detox, all those toxins from modern life being flushed out with the aid of your favourite drink. And to avoid dehydration drink some neat H_2O after a session.

To quote a phrase attributed to sixteenth-century Swiss physician Paracelsus: '*Cerevisia malorum divina medicina.*' ('A little bit of beer is divine medicine.')

Social welfare

Beer is the most convivial of drinks and makes people happy, which is beneficial for general well-being, and physical and mental health. Professor Sheldon Cohen, Professor of Psychology at Carnegie Mellon University in the USA, said, 'We need to take more seriously the possibility that a positive emotional style is a major player in disease risk.'

Beer helps to build social bonds – just look around the pub to see that in action as people, formerly strangers, start chatting over a pint. Britain's first pubs were alehouses and even today a pub is not really a pub unless it sells beer. Pubs are at the core of British society where people, regardless of background, come together to enjoy the national drink and have a communal good time; after-work drinks down the pub are another example of friendships being cemented over beer. There is a reason why British soap operas set so many scenes in the Rovers, Queen Vic and Woolpack – all life happens in the boozer: relationships are formed, love affairs and celebrations conducted, arguments (and make-ups) developed, business conducted, deals sealed. The pub offers a refuge, companionship, entertainment – and beer is at the centre of it all.

The health benefits of a good social life are not to be underestimated. In a report published in March 2013 in the Proceedings of the National Academy of Sciences, lead research professor Andrew Steptoe, Director of the Institute of Epidemiology and Health Care at University College London, stated:

Social contact is a fundamental aspect of human existence. The scientific evidence is that being socially isolated is probably bad for your health, and may lead to the development of serious illness and a reduced life span.

So stay happy and healthy with the help of a glass of your favourite beer down the boozer with your mates!

BEER AS MEDICINE

Historically, a variety of plants, herbs and spices were added to beer for their tonic and medicinal properties. They included:

Alder bark and buds: they help to stop diarrhoea.

Aloes: used for their purging nature.

Bishop's wort: a cure for fever.

Bogbean: thought to prevent scurvy. In large doses it was used to purge the digestive system.

Chamomile: has gentle laxative properties.

Coltsfoot: is a good remedy for coughs.

Common ash: purges the stomach as a laxative and diuretic, and promotes perspiration.

Cowslip: cures dizziness, and relieves stress.

Elecampane: herbalist Nicholas Culpeper said it '*cleareth, strengtheneth, and quickeneth the sight of the eyes*'.

Eyebright: thought to improve sight.

Hyssop: used as an expectorant (helps bring mucus from the lungs) and to calm flatulence.

Nettles: used to treat rheumatic and gout pains.

Watercress and wild carrot: thought to prevent scurvy.

Wood betony: used to treat headaches. Chewing the leaves before drinking was thought to prevent drunkenness.

Specific medical ales were also brewed in England to treat various ailments:

'Buttered beere' was a medieval concoction that contained butter, sugar, two egg yolks and grated ginger; it was believed to be good for shortness of breath and coughs.

Some alehouses prepared tonic ale by soaking a cheesecloth bag containing sarsaparilla, senna pods and other herbs in the cask. The ale was drunk to promote healthy lungs and stomach, and to prevent indigestion and colds.

Saxons believed that the devil was the cause of many health problems. A way to fight 'fiend-sickness' was to add mixed herbs, garlic and holy water to ale and drink it out of an inverted church bell after several masses had been said for the patient.

Feast – Matching Beer With Food

A quart of ale is a dish for a king.
William Shakespeare, *The Winter's Tale*, Act IV, Scene III

Recently on Twitter someone asked the question, 'Is beer the new wine when it comes to matching with food?' Well no, actually, wine is the new beer. It is little more than a century since beer ceased to be consumed with every meal and throughout history millions more people have had beer on the table than they have had wine. King Henry VIII and Queen Elizabeth I were partial to ale and, like most people in those times, drank it throughout the day and with food too.

In recent years, the wine industry's PR efforts seem to have been more effective than those of beer; the perception that wine is a high-status libation while beer is for the common folk has meant that beer is ignored when it comes to 'fine dining'. But having that attitude about beer leads to missing out on some of the most complex and flavoursome drinking/dining experiences you may ever have. Being a beer sommelier, I would say that. Still, in the interests of research I have drunk plenty of wine with food too, but to me beer with food wins hands down each time.

I find beer so much more versatile, diverse and forgiving. I once had the temerity to pop a piece of fish finger in my mouth and then take a sip of a spicy South African Shiraz. The wine formed a devilish alliance with the phosphate in the fish and it latched on to my fillings, coating my mouth with a horrible metallic taste. Beer would never have done that – offering instead a friendly greeting to the fish and thanking it for visiting. And another thing about beer: it will happily match with every dish in every meal of the day, whether vegetarian, fish, or meat, breakfast and dessert included. Wine cannot do that with such panache.

So why is beer perfect for matching with food? For flavour and texture, but also for the practical fact that beer is up to 95 per cent water so it refreshes the mouth, and that is the number one reason why we want liquid with our food. Beer contains carbon dioxide, an efficient scrubber that prepares the mouth by clearing the palate to make it ready, willing and able for the next morsel. Even real ale with no discernible bubbles contains dissolved CO_2, which adds a note of invigorating acidity and lightens the richness of food. And remembering how important aroma is when appreciating food and drink, CO_2 elevates the beer's aromas from the glass to the nose and starts a luscious anticipation of what is to come.

Where wine has acidity and tannins, beer has hops. Hops are bitter – some more than others – and bitterness is refreshing. The sharpness of hops acts like a knife cutting through flavour and texture, so a beer where hops are in the ascendant will be a good choice when faced with a big creamy, fatty or heavily spiced dish.

When pairing beer with food this is a useful mantra: cut, complement or contrast. You can choose which of those roles the beer should perform.

Cut: choose a beer that cuts through the flavour or body of the food. For instance, fish and chips require a crisp refreshing beer to cut through fat, and citrus hops to complement the fish.

Complement: choose a beer that will complement the flavours of the food. For instance, spicy food goes with a beer containing spicy hops.

Contrast: choose a beer that is a complete contrast to the food. For instance, big-flavoured chocolatey porter or stout contrasts well with salty Stilton.

But rules can be broken and it is fun to experiment to see which beers work with certain dishes. So 'goodbye wine' and 'hello beer' at your next dinner party. Here are some tips for wowing the guests:

For an aperitif serve light, zesty beer in a Champagne flute. There are two brands that are so light drinkers often do not realise they are drinking beer: 'Kasteel Cru' and 'DeuS'.

Depending on the menu, start with lighter-bodied beers, and move onto bigger-bodied beers throughout the meal. Offer a different beer with each course in a variety of glassware such as wine glasses and brandy goblets.

If in doubt, match the colour of the beer to the food. For instance, grilled fish or chicken with pale-coloured beer such as wheat, Pilsner, or golden ale.

A successful rule for beer and food pairings is to match flavour intensity: delicate with delicate, spice with spice, big with big. But contrasts can work beautifully too.

Consider the texture of the food when choosing the beer – light texture such as sushi with lighter-bodied beers. The more solid the food, such as hearty stews, the bigger the body of the beer.

Match the beer with the main part of the dish rather than the trimmings – so with a Sunday roast, pair the meat and not the vegetables. Ignore that rule, however, with spicy Indian or creamy food because hops and acidity are required to counter the flavour (with spices) and to cut through the fat (with cream).

Consider how the food is cooked. Grilled or roasted meat and vegetables, for example, will usually be caramelised and beers with a malty caramel flavour profile match well. Charred food such as barbeque will find a friend in the burnt malts of porter or stout.

Dessert matches should really intrigue your guests. Surely beer cannot possibly go with sweet food? Oh my, what a treat this will be. Choose more than one dessert and then hit them with a range of beers such as those suggested in 'A Day of Beer and Food Matching' below.

Vegetarians, do not despair: there is much fun to be had conjuring up beer menus. Overseas cuisines come into their own here. Chinese with German Weizen or smoked beer; Indian with hoppy pale ale or crisp Pilsners or Helles; Lebanese with India pale ale or Märzen; Mexican with brown ale or smoked beer; Thai with Belgian witbier or strong golden ale; Vietnamese with saison or Belgian witbier. Mushroom dishes go well with earthy beers and those with high caramel and nutty characters such as brown ale, Doppelbocks and Dunkels. Then there is the magnificence of cheese to consider (see 'Cheese' below for some great pairings).

A Day of Beer and Food Matching

If any proof were needed as to the versatility of beer as a match for food, here are some suggestions of what to drink with each meal of the day:

Breakfast:

Porridge: golden honey ale such as Organic Heather Honey Beer by Black Isle.

Kedgeree: India pale ale such as Shoreditch Triangle IPA by London Fields Brewery.

Scrambled eggs: Kölsch such as Kölsch by Früh.

Full English: malty ale such as Junction by Sambrook's Brewery.

Elevenses:

Or, as the Germans say, *Brotzeit* (a second breakfast that translates as 'bread time') or *zweites Frühstück* (mid-morning snack), when it is customary to sneak in a cheeky beer. Wheat beer is restorative in that stretch before lunch – for instance, Weisse Original by Maisel traditionally matched with a sausage or pretzel. Visit a Bavarian beer hall around 11 a.m. and it will usually be full.

Lunch:

Salad Niçoise: witbier such as St Bernardus Blanche by St Bernardus Brouwerij.

Cheese and pickle sandwich: bitter such as Alton's Pride by Triple fff Brewery.

Sushi: Pilsner such as Pilsner by Veltins.

Grilled chicken: Belgian pale ale such as Duvel by Brouwerij De Koninck.

Spotted dick and custard: Altbier such as Alt by Uerige Obergärige Hausbrauerei.

Afternoon tea:
Smoked salmon sandwiches followed by scones and clotted cream: gueuze such as Oude Gueuze by Mort Subite.

Dinner:
Vegetable masala: saison such as India Saison by Nøgne Ø.
Tapas: Helles such as Freakin' Helles by Brewster's Brewing Company.
Lobster: Flanders red ale such as Grand Cru by Rodenbach.
Game: Trappist such as La Trappe Quadrupel by De Koningshoeven.
Brandy snaps and whipped cream: something containing subtle ginger such as Blandford Flyer by Badger.
Instead of Cognac after dinner treat your taste buds to a glass of Fuller's Vintage Ale. This extraordinary beer deserves to be genuflected to before pouring. It is a barley wine (8.5% ABV) brewed once a year and, because it is bottle-conditioned, it will age over time. Choose a vintage that is at least two years older than the date on the label so it has aged.

Dessert:
'Beer and dessert? You're 'aving a giraffe, mate!' There is so much fun to be had disabusing people who have that opinion. Think of some of the flavours in beer – biscuit, caramel, toffee, vanilla, nuts, aniseed, honey, fruit, coffee, chocolate. All of them are also found on the pudding menu. Hungry yet? Here is a guide to sweet-noshing nirvana.

Dessert: apple pie or crumble.
Beer: imperial Russian stout such as Black Chocolate Stout by Brooklyn Brewery; or Ebulum Elderberry Black Ale by Williams Brothers.

Dessert: banana split.
Beer: wheat such as Weissbier by Erdinger; or porter such as Gonzo Imperial Porter by Flying Dog.

Dessert: Black Forest gateau.
Beer: Belgian fruit beer such as Kriek by Liefmans; or Frambozen by Bacchus.

Dessert: Christmas pudding.
Beer: barley wine or old ale such as Old Guardian Barley Wine by Stone Brewing Company; or Owd Rodger by Marston's.

Dessert: chocolate brownies.
Beer: stout or porter such as Old Engine Oil by Harviestoun; or Plum Porter by Titanic.

Dessert: coffee and walnut cake.
Beer: Dunkel or brown ale such as Dunkel by Brauereigasthof Rothenbach Aufsesser; or Stokey Brown by Pressure Drop.

Dessert: crème brûlée.
Beer: oak-aged beer or Doppelbock such as Rum Cask by Innis & Gunn; or Asam Bock by Weltenburger Kloster.

Dessert: fruit tart.
Beer: beers with subtle fruit character such as Golden Glory by Badger; or Rosé by Kasteel Cru.

Dessert: ice cream.
Beer: stout or Belgian fruit beers such as Triple Chocoholic by Saltaire; Kriek Mariage Parfait by Boon.

Dessert: mince pies.
Beer: stout pale or Doppelbock, for instance White Stout by Durham Brewery; Bajuvator Doppelbock by Tucher Bräu Fürth.

Dessert: nuts.
Beer: dubbel or mild such as Dubbel by Westmalle; or Ruby Mild by Sarah Hughes Brewery.

Dessert: rice pudding.
Beer: oak-aged or abbey beer such as Original Oak Aged Beer by Innis & Gunn; or Bon Secours Brune by La Brasserie Caulier.

Dessert: rich fruit cake.
Beer: old ale or barley wine such as Tally-Ho by Adnams Brewery; or Skull Splitter by The Orkney Brewery.

Dessert: tiramisu.
Beer: stout such as Double Stout by Shepherd Neame; or Ultimate Stout by Bristol Beer Factory.

Dessert: treacle tart.
Beers: oak-aged such as Winter Treacle Porter by Innis & Gunn; or Ola Dubh (aged in whisky barrels) by Harviestoun.

When it comes to dessert, then, there are several beer styles that really stand out. Stout and porter with their coffee and chocolate characters are winners, and the brands in the Innis & Gunn range of oak-aged beers are spectacular. Of all the beers I have ever matched with food, the latter are the most versatile. So for the author's special accolade of Supreme Food Beer Award of the Millennium raise a glass to Innis & Gunn, because their beers go with smoked fish, smoked meat, mild curry, roast lamb, countless types of cheese and myriad desserts – and they are brilliant on their own!

Cheese:

But now, for the pièce de résistance: the cheese. Beer and cheese were made for each other. Wine and cheese is a polite cohabitation; beer and cheese is a passionate union. Beer and cheese have much in common, not least because they acquire so much of their character through the microflora that ferment them. They also share a plethora of flavours and textures such as fruity, nutty, toasty, earthy, grainy, savoury, creamy, sweet, acidic, spicy, tangy and herbal.

Try these suggestions:

Cheese: soft and creamy such as Bath Soft, Brie, l'Explorateur
Beer: well-hopped pale ales such as Hop A Doodle Doo by Brewster's Brewing Company, or fruit beers such as Raspberry by Meantime Brewery.
Why? These cheeses and beers have similar levels of acidity, and the crisp textures of the beer, the hops and the fruit are a foil for the creaminess of the cheese.

Cheese: Brillat-Savarin or Vignotte
Beer: Pilsner such as English Lager by St Peter's, or Helles such as Hells by Camden Town Brewery.
Why? Creamy cheese needs a crisp, acidic, well-hopped beer.

Cheese: goat's cheese or Wensleydale
Beer: wheat beer such as Weisse Original by Schneider & Sohn; or Flanders red ale such as Duchesse de Bourgogne by Brouwerij Verhaeghe.
Why? Tartness is characteristic of the cheeses and both beers are tart, tangy and fruity.

Cheese: Caerphilly
Beer: saison such as Saison by Dupont.
Why? The cheese is fresh and creamy with a bright acidity that complements saison beers on account of their dry and citrus characteristics.

Cheese: Cornish Yarg
Beer: Belgian witbier such as Hoegaarden.
Why? Cornish Yarg has a tangy citrus taste that is lifted by the lemony and spiced character of the beer.

Cheese: Cheddar, Lincolnshire Poacher
Beer: malty bitter such as Broadside by Adnams; or brown ale such as 09/02 Nut Brown Ale by Brew by Numbers.
Why? These are savoury, nutty, salty cheeses so big, rich, complex, sweet, caramel, malty beers are a contrast.

Cheese: Emmentaler, Gouda
Beer: Märzen or oak-aged beer such as Oktober Fest-Märzen by Brauerei Aying; or Original Oak Aged Beer by Innis & Gunn.
Why? Rich, toasted caramel, toffee-flavoured beer contrasts well with savoury, nutty cheese.

Cheese: Alderwood, Gruyère
Beer: dark mild such as Nutty Black by Thwaites Brewery.
Why? Dark milds are nutty with an underlying sweetness that is a perfect partner for mildly flavoured, sweetly nutty cheese.

Cheese: Double Gloucester
Beer: bières de gardes such as Brasseurs Bière de Garde by Brouwerij Huyghe.
Why? Nutty savoury cheese matches well with beers with pronounced toasted malt and sweet caramel flavours.

Cheese: Pecorino Tartufo
Beer: Orval by Brasserie d'Orval.
Why? Such a singular beer as Orval deserves an equally singular cheese. This one is studded with truffles that impart an unmistakable aroma. Orval is a dry and earthy beer of enormous complexity. Serve this combination and your guests will be in raptures.

Cheese: Manchego
Beer: old ale such as Old Tom by Robinsons Brewery.
Why? Full-flavoured and full-bodied beers with sweet, nutty, treacle characters are a joy with a savoury cheese with hints of caramel and hazelnut.

Cheese: Vacherin
Beer: India pale ale such as Halcyon by Thornbridge.
Why? The soft, buttery, earthy cheese needs a big zesty beer. India pale ale also matches beautifully with blue cheese, the hops making magic with the mould, and also cheeses with high cream content when the hops cut right through the fat and refresh the mouth.

Cheese: Gorgonzola, Roquefort, Stilton
Beer: porter and imperial Russian stout such as Midnight Sun by Williams Brothers, or Imperial Russian Stout by Courage.
Why? This is all about huge flavours. Blue cheese has a funky, salty and earthy character that meets big-bodied, malty, aromatic, roasted chocolate and coffee-flavoured beer with strapping enthusiasm and on equal terms of impact.

Cheese: Cashel Blue, Cornish Blue
Beer: barley wine such as Golden Pride by Fuller's.
Why? This match is about contrast – salty, funky cheese with a big smooth, sweetish caramel beer.

Cheese: raclette
Beer: Rauchbier such as Rauchbier Märzen by Aecht Schlenkerla, or smoked porter such as Smoked Porter by Stone Brewing Company.
Why? Both beers have smoked flavours that enhance the nutty and slightly smoky character of the cheese.

Cheese: Abbaye de Trois Vaux
Beer: Trappist beers such as Bleue by Chimay.
Why? The rind of the cheese is washed in beer and the hops penetrate the cheese. Heaven. It is also nutty and savoury so a big sweet caramel beer such as Chimay will contrast well.

Beers That Ruled the World

Three beer styles dominate the past four hundred years of brewing: Pilsner lager, pale ale and porter (which includes stout). They have been so influential they are now brewed around the world, far from their original homes.

Pilsner lager

Versions of Pilsner are brewed in every country of the world where alcohol is legal, and approximately 90 per cent of all beer consumed worldwide falls into the pale 'lager' category. Unfortunately, many of the brands are quite often tasteless, highly carbonated, watery and do not hit the spot. They give Pilsner a bad name. At best, however, this style of beer is crisp and sharp, with a refreshing spiky bitterness that does not disguise the gorgeous sweet malts. It is the ultimate international beer and connects drinkers in São Paulo with counterparts in Shanghai; Melbourne with Miami.

But where did this superstar beer style originate? Both Germany and the Czech Republic can lay claim to it, with some technological input from England. The word itself, Pilsner, derives from a town in the Czech Republic called Pilsen. Beer lovers in that town were already keen on beers from over the border in Bavaria made using lager yeast – a hybrid that evolved from two yeast species, *Saccharomyces cerevisiae* and *Saccharomyces bayanus* – which fermented at cool temperatures.

Cool-fermenting beers were nothing new in Germany, where for centuries Bavarian brewers had fermented their beer in cool caves or dark underground tunnels to protect it against spoiling in summer heat. Though German brewers were adept at warm-fermenting beers such as Weizen and Altbier, it was the yeast for their cool-fermenting Dunkels and Bocks that became the inspiration for the new style of beer brewed in Pilsen. The local burghers wanted to capitalise on the demand for beer by building their own brewery rather than importing beer from Germany. Lager yeast was purchased from Germany, and English-style maltings were installed. 'English style' meant that the barley was malted using indirect heat, rather than malting over wood, therefore pale malts were possible, untainted with smoky flavours from the fuel. In 1842 the brewery was ready to make an innovative style of crisp and refreshing beer. It was called Pilsner Urquell.

So German yeast and English malting techniques, brewed with passion in the Czech Republic, made the first pale lager possible – a collaboration of brewing knowledge that gave the world its favourite beer style.

British beerios will remember how pale lager became *the* fashionable beer in the 1970s and seduced a generation of younger people who did not want to drink what their parents did i.e. old-fashioned ale. Lager brewers heavily marketed their brands (and still do) with characters such as the Hofmeister bear. And who can forget the genius advertising strapline of 'I bet he drinks Carling Black Label'? Millions of British drinkers and brewers joined the lager love-in. Even the venerable Fuller, Smith & Turner introduced a lager – K2 (long discontinued) – to their range.

But lager was not a new beer in Britain. It was already being brewed in Scotland in 1835 using cool-fermenting yeast from

Bavaria. Other nineteenth-century brewers started producing lager, but ale brewers retaliated to the threat by brewing lower-alcohol, lighter, paler beers. It was only in the mid to late twentieth century that lager overtook ale as the most popular style of beer in Britain.

GERMAN ESPIONAGE

At the heart of lager history are two German James Bonds (or *Null Null Siebens*, as 007s are referred to in dubbed German versions of the films) – Gabriel Sedlmayr and Anton Dreher. Both scions of major brewing families, together in 1837 they travelled around Europe on the beer equivalent of the Grand Tour, visiting numerous breweries to learn new techniques in order to improve their own beers. In Britain they learned about malting techniques and how brewers used various implements such as saccharometers to measure the sugar in the brew. Some of their knowledge came from discussions with brewers but in certain cases what they wanted to know was commercially sensitive and that meant employing the underhand techniques of industrial espionage. Both men carried hollow walking sticks fitted with valves so they could surreptitiously plunge them into fermenting vessels and fill the stick with beer and yeast to take away for later analysis. Sedlmayr and Dreher took what they had learned about British brewing back home and, with their existing Bavarian brewing expertise and cool-fermenting yeasts, started to brew paler beers that eventually inspired the development of Pilsner.

WHAT HAPPENED TO MY TASTE, BUD?

Many mainstream American lager-style beers are light and easy-drinking. Blame Prohibition and the Great Depression for establishing in so many American palates a fear of flavour. Most of the biggest breweries in the nineteenth century had been established by German immigrants to the USA, many of whom brewed their favourite style of beer from the home country – pale lager. By the 1910s more beer was produced in America than anywhere else in the world. When prohibition of alcohol became law in 1920, breweries were forced to close or brew 'near beer', which, without alcohol, would have been lacklustre.

This state of affairs lasted for thirteen years until the law was repealed. But in the years of Prohibition people had forgotten what a tasty beer was; they had become used to soft drinks, and many young people had grown into adults without ever having tasted beer. Those factors, plus stipulations that banned alcohol in beer higher than 4% ABV, led in only one direction – bland.

The Great Depression added further constraints. Brewers were obliged to keep prices low, which meant reducing the amount of expensive malted barley in favour of cheap alternatives such as corn and rice. To cut production costs even further, the pricey aging process of the beer had to go. American lager bore no resemblance to what it had been fifty years prior but there were few people around to remember that, so drinkers just accepted that beer was supposed to be low on flavour, and millions of them have done so ever since. Yet some of the tastiest beers on earth are now being brewed by small independents in America. So next time a bottle of Sierra Nevada Torpedo IPA is cracked open, consider this – without the blandification of mainstream American beers in the post-Prohibition years, maybe the craft beer revolution would never have happened.

FAR EAST BREWS

The Snow lager brand is currently the world's biggest-selling beer – but it is mostly consumed in the country it is brewed in, China. Brewing in China was introduced in the early twentieth century when German brewers set up business there – hence the popularity of Pilsner-style lager.

By contrast, one of the world's lower-selling beers, Taedong River Beer (a pale lager), is brewed in North Korea and dubbed the 'Pride of Pyongyang'. It is made in second-hand brewing equipment purchased in 2000 for £1.5 million from Usher's Brewery in Trowbridge in Wiltshire.

Pale ale

What determines the shade of beer? The type of malt used for brewing it. And the colour of malt is determined by the source of heat used in the malting process. The earliest beers would most likely have been pale as the malt was dried by sunlight. Even with Britain's climate where cloud cover is common, sun-dried malts would have been a possibility, so early Britons would have been downing a pottle or two of pale-coloured ale – though sadly they could not appreciate the glorious hue because most drinking vessels until the nineteenth century were made from wood, leather or pewter. Until 1845, when Excise Duty on glass was dropped and mass-production techniques significantly reduced the cost, most beer drinkers were unable to quaff from a glass, so the colour and clarity of beer were not all that important.

When wood, straw and peat started to be used as fuel, dark malts were produced, and consequently brown, mahogany and black beers could be brewed; but as those fuels directly heated the barley, the malt would have had a smoky character that infused the beer. Coke, the coal-derived fuel, was invented in northern England in the early seventeenth century and by 1640 maltsters in Derbyshire were using it to produce pale malts that had no smokiness, just the pure, sweet, biscuit character. Britain's inland waterways transported this pale malt to brewers around the country, and with increased availability of coke other maltsters were able to supply similar malts, so pale ale was already being widely brewed before Burton-upon-Trent became celebrated for that particular style in the nineteenth century. But the confluence of pale ale's increasing popularity with the development of the railways in the nineteenth century meant the leading brewers such as Bass could distribute their pale ale to a wider market. When St Pancras station was constructed in 1866, the building dimensions of the undercroft (now used by Eurostar) were measured to the millimetre because it was a storage warehouse for barrels of beer that had arrived in the city on trains from the major brewing hub of Burton-upon-Trent.

India pale ale (IPA) was one of the first international beers and the esteem it garnered not just in India but also imperial Russia gave it status as a fashionable libation. As previously mentioned, IPA was originally known as October ale, so renaming it India pale ale was one of the first beer branding exercises. It was a marketing masterstroke for a beer to be named after the jewel in the crown of the British Empire.

Tastes change and as the demand for dark, malty, heavy porter slowly waned in the nineteenth century, the lighter-coloured and highly hopped pale ale grew in popularity. It was nicknamed 'bitter' and that moniker stuck. If there is a symbol to illustrate Britain's love affair with beer, it is a pint of bitter.

Today English style pale ale is brewed in several countries, particularly ones that have former colonial ties with Britain – USA, South Africa, Australia and New Zealand.

HOW PALE IS PALE?

Pale ale comes in a variety of colours – straw, yellow, amber, copper – some of them not all that pale. So why the term 'pale ale'? Because compared to other beers of the eighteenth century that were brown or mahogany, it was indeed pale ale.

Porter

Method-acting guide for Charles Dickens' characters: blacken the teeth, use a crutch, stick on a facial carbuncle, then order a plate of oysters and wash them down with a tankard of porter.

Porter is largely associated with Britain in the nineteenth century but the beer first appeared in the early eighteenth century and even before Dickens was born it was consumed around the world. Captain Cook carried barrels of it in 1768 aboard his ship *Endeavour* during a voyage of exploration to the Pacific. When a penal colony was established in Sydney, Australia in 1788, officers on the first ships to arrive toasted their safe passage with porter carried with them from London. Expats in India drank it as a taste of home, and Americans were also partial, even after independence. In Ireland, it was all the rage.

Porter started off as brown ale – dark, sweet, malty and heavy – the principal beer of London brewers up to the beginning of the eighteenth century. When pale, highly hopped beers started to threaten the dominance of brown ale, something had to be done. The beer had a makeover: with more hops, and longer fermentation and maturation, it became drier, less sweet, and as it aged acquired a tart, fruity quality.

At first this redesigned beer was known as 'Entire Butt' (from the fact that the malt was mashed several times and the worts blended in big brewery casks known as butts), but as it became the essential drink of the working man of the streets it acquired the nickname 'porter', first mentioned in writing in 1721. The river and street porters who carried goods around London, or loaded and unloaded freight from ships and carts, needed plenty of water and energy and the best source was beer from the numerous pubs in the capital – and that's how it got its name. By the nineteenth century more porter was being brewed than any other beer and London was the world's leading brewing city.

Nowadays most people would think of stout as being dark but when the term was first used to describe beer (around 1630) it meant strong. So any higher-alcohol version of a beer, even pale, could be described as 'stout'. Stout porter was just one version of porter. The others were common porter, best porter, double stout and imperial Russian stout – a style of beer that was exported to the imperial court in St Petersburg.

The best-known purveyor of stout is Guinness. Arthur Guinness started off as a small-time brewer and got in on the act when London porter imports proved enormously popular in Dublin. He started brewing his own local version of the beer and by 1799 decided to specialise in porter only and eschew other styles. In the nineteenth century Guinness started brewing beers with a high proportion of unmalted roasted barley that gave the beer an opaque black hue and a distinctive charred quality. It was called Extra Stout Porter and it set the taste profile for what Guinness is today – dry and with a significant burned character.

> ## THE BLACK STUFF
>
> Arthur Guinness's commitment to his craft was obvious when in 1759 he took a 9,000-year lease on the brewery site at St James's Gate. Guinness now produces 1.8 billion pints of stout annually and sells it in over a hundred countries. The five top-selling markets for Guinness are, in order: Britain, Ireland, Nigeria, USA and Cameroon. Not bad for a brewer who paid £100 when he signed the contract on the brewery (using the retail prices index to calculate the worth in today's money, it would be approximately £12,000), with an additional £45 per annum rent.

Desert island beers

A common question among beer lovers is 'What's your favourite beer?' With so many superb beers in the world I find it impossible to decide but when asked I usually respond, 'It depends on my mood, situation and the weather' – which is another way of saying 'all good beer'. Imagine the hell of being stranded on a desert island with only a limited supply of beer. If that ever happened I would pray to Ninkasi that a shipping container full of beer crates and a chalice or tulip glass followed in my wake. I would take heart that, despite there being no pub, I had a stash of some of my best-loved beers. These are in alphabetical order:

BBC 2 by Brentwood Brewing Company (Brentwood, Essex)

Historically 'small beer' was low-strength ale consumed by all the family as a safe source of water when H_2O might be polluted with all manner of poisonous substances. BBC 2 is 2.5% ABV but there is nothing small about this beer. Full of aroma, flavour and character, this will be the beer I turn to every morning upon waking on the desert island.

Black Cat Mild by Moorhouse's Brewery (Burnley, Lancashire)

When I was fifteen I had my first pint – Tetley Mild – and it was instant devotion. So to remind me of why I fell in love with beer, this classic mild and former Supreme Champion Beer of Britain will keep me happy.

Duchesse de Bourgogne by Verhaeghe (Vichte, West-Vlaanderen, Belgium)

This is a beer I often dream about with its tangy, sour, almost wine-like character. On the palate it has a sherbet quality and it is unlike any other beer I know. As variety is the spice of life, the Duchesse will tingle my taste buds with her sassy concoction when I need a pick-me-up.

Myrcenary Double IPA by Odell Brewing Company (Fort Collins, Colorado, USA)

Once I had recovered from the shock of paying £15 for two small bottles of this beer in a London pub to share with four friends, I raised the snifter glass to my nose and suddenly I was transported to a grove of the most aromatic tropical fruits, including pineapples and tangerines. It was my second experience of a double IPA (hops, hops and more hops) – Torpedo by Sierra Nevada being the first – and I have never forgotten it. Dangerously drinkable though – it hides its 9.3% ABV very well indeed.

Ola Dubh (12 year old) by Harviestoun Brewery (Alva, Clackmannanshire)

Imperial Russian stout is an intense style of beer in body and flavour, and perfect for people who like liquid burned rubber. If that sounds off-putting, good – more for me! Some beers are 'one bottle only per night' and Ola Dubh (it translates as 'Black Oil' in Scots Gaelic) is that for me, with its huge, rich, dark chocolate, treacle, full-bodied personality, tinged with distinctive flavours of whisky from the 'Highland Park 12 year old' barrels in which the beer is aged. I have stunned so many wine drinkers with Ola Dubh who were not aware of what gargantuan flavours and complexity can be found in beer. The reason I will not drink more than one bottle in a sitting is that this beer is so perfect, I want to ration myself so that I will never say, 'Oh, not that one again.' As Scarlett O'Hara commented in *Gone with the Wind*, 'After all, tomorrow is another day', and I can look forward to the following evening to open another bottle of this extraordinary brew.

Pale Ale by Brewster's Brewing Company (Grantham, Lincolnshire)

After an arduous day building sandcastles on my desert island I will need refreshment, and what better way to perk up the palate that with some hops? This beer is often also the first beer I turn to after work back in the real world. It is crisp and fresh with a grapefruit finish, and oh so moreish. Pass another bottle please.

Vintage Ale by Fuller, Smith & Turner (London)

I am partial to barley wine – those strong, full-bodied beers with a solid, malty backbone – and to me there is none better than Fuller's Vintage Ale. This limited-edition beer is brewed once a year, then bottle-conditioned and left to age. Seven years of maturation is my ideal, when the caramel malt has formed a passionate alliance with Fuller's unique citrus-fruit-aroma yeast and spicy lemon English hops to create a marmalade fantasy in the guise of a beer. Vintage Ale comes in a cardboard presentation box so when I have ten empties I will set the boxes up on the beach and play skittles with a coconut. Much easier to knock over than bottles!

It will not take me long to drink all these incredible beers so please send a rescue party soon.

Supreme Champion Beers of Britain

Each year at the Great British Beer Festival, one beer is crowned Supreme Champion Beer of Britain. The beers are judged blind and win or lose on their merits. CAMRA organises the festival and finding the winning beer involves months of research beforehand by trained tasting panels around the country. The judges are made aware beforehand of the styles of beer they are to taste and score them on colour, clarity, aroma, flavour, body, overall drinking experience, and whether they are good representations of the style. From hundreds of beers the nominees are reduced to a short list. On the first day of the festival a group of experts taste the final beers to decide on the overall winner.

So if you want to sample the best of the best, these are the first dozen winners since 2000 (in reverse order):

2012

Name: No. 9 Barley Wine by Coniston Brewing Company (Coniston, Cumbria)
Style: Barley wine
ABV: 8.5%
Colour: Chestnut
Description: A big-bodied, dried fruit, treacle, honey, vinous, and sherry-like beer.

2011

Name: Oscar Wilde by Mighty Oak (Maldon, Essex)
Style: Mild
ABV: 3.7%
Colour: Ruby
Description: Sweetish toffee, toasted bread, light chocolate flavour, low bitterness.

2010

Name: Harvest Pale by Castle Rock (Nottingham)
Style: Blonde ale
ABV: 3.8%
Colour: Pale golden
Description: Tangy, fruity, medium bitterness, dry finish.

2009

Name: Ruby Mild by Rudgate (York, North Yorkshire)
Style: Mild
ABV: 4.4%
Colour: Dark copper
Description: Toasted caramel and nuts, rich and malty, bitter finish.

2008
Name: Alton's Pride by Triple fff (Alton, Hampshire)
Style: Bitter
ABV: 3.8%
Colour: Amber
Description: Soft fruits, citrus, honey, bitter dry finish.

2007
Name: Mild by Hobsons (Cleobury Mortimer, Worcestershire)
Style: Mild
ABV: 3.2%
Colour: Mahogany
Description: Chocolate, nuts, caramel sweetness, light bitterness.

2006 and 2005 (the same beer won two years running)
Name: Brewers Gold by Crouch Vale (South Woodham Ferrers, Essex)
Style: Pale ale
ABV: 4%
Colour: Golden
Description: Honey, citrus, tropical fruit, spicy bitter hop finish.

2004
Name: Pale Rider by Kelham Island (Sheffield, South Yorkshire)
Style: Pale ale
ABV: 5.2%
Colour: Golden
Description: Peaches, citrus, caramel and biscuit, floral bitter finish.

2003

Name: Bitter & Twisted by Harviestoun (Alva, Clackmannanshire)
Style: Blonde ale
ABV: 4.2%
Colour: Golden
Description: Herbal, pine, citrus, caramel and biscuit, bitter finish.

2002

Name: Deuchars IPA by Caledonian (Edinburgh)
Style: Bitter
ABV: 3.8%
Colour: Copper gold
Description: Apples and peach, toasted caramel, medium bitterness.

2001

Name: JHB (Jeffery Hudson Bitter) by Oakham Ales (Peterborough, Cambridgeshire)
Style: Bitter
ABV: 3.8%
Colour: Golden
Description: Biscuit, soft fruit, citrus, grassy, dry bitter finish.

2000

Name: Black Cat by Moorhouse's (Burnley, Lancashire)
Style: Mild
ABV: 3.4%
Colour: Mahogany
Description: Caramel, roasted malt, chocolate, coffee, dry medium bitter finish.

Great Brewing Nations of the World

Beer is brewed in almost every country where alcohol is legal, but only a handful of nations can claim to have influenced the rest of the world with the beer styles they developed or adopted – or to have become famous for their beer culture. Here they are, in alphabetical order:

Australia

There is a burgeoning craft beer scene down under, but Aussie drinkers are still most associated with downing gallons of ultra-chilled carbonated pale lagers. The style was first brewed in 1886 when two brothers, William and Ralph Foster, arrived from New York accompanied by a German brewer and a refrigeration engineer who would ensure a supply of ice for all stockists of the soon-to-be-brewed beer. Goodbye to Old Country beers such as porter and hello to the perfect beer for the hot Australian climate – Pilsner.

Belgium

Is there another brewing nation that earns so much respect, passion and pilgrimage as Belgium? Bars in Bruges and Brussels are temples of beer worship with hundreds of choices on the menu. Heaven on earth – unless you happen to be a hophead (try British and American brews instead). Belgian brewers do use hops but usually for gentle bittering and for their preservative quality rather than aromatic heft. It is no insult to say that most Belgian beers are not subtle – big aroma and even bigger flavour. From the effervescent Brut des Flandres matured like Champagne, the shockingly tart gueuze, tangy fruit beers such as Kriek and Frambozen, and refreshing and fortifying strong Belgian ales such as Duvel, to the sweet and seriously complex Trappist ales such as Chimay and Westmalle, they show off the diversity of brewing in a spectacular way with a range of ales that are unmistakably Belgian.

Belgium can also claim to be progenitor of one of the branches in the family tree of beer – Lambic. Beers classified as Lambic are fermented with wild yeast and other microflora that give an unmistakable funky, sour character to the beer. Brewers in other countries make Lambics but for an authentic example visit a bar in the Senne valley outside Brussels and order one of the local beers.

Belgian beers are an excellent way of converting people who think they do not like beer. Usually it is bitterness or clunky glassware that puts off some people, particularly women, from drinking beer. Few Belgian beers are bitter – some are sweetish, others are fruity or sour. And in Belgium customers are usually presented with their drink in an elegant stemmed chalice or tulip-type glass.

Even mainstream Stella Artois (one of the biggest-selling beers in the world) is served in its own special chalice. Bar staff are trained to be expert in the pouring ritual and can enter an international competition to win the World Draught Masters Championship.

Britain

Cask-conditioned ale is the traditional British way of serving beer. With this method of dispensing, where the ale is pulled through pipes from a cask by the action of pumping a handle on the bar, the soul of the beer, yeast, remains working – maintaining flavour and freshness.

Brewers in Britain can claim to have invented more styles of beer regularly brewed around the world than any other brewing nation – barley wine, brown ale, golden ale, India pale ale, mild, pale ale, porter and stout. Another gold star on British brewing's progress report is the ability to make satisfying, highly flavoured, low-alcohol session beers. Alcohol gives flavour to beer so when it is in low levels, the taste has to come from elsewhere. Thanks to top quality, flavoursome British barley malts and hops, and the brewers' skills, even a beer of 3.2% ABV – that's low – has enough character to win the accolade of Supreme Champion Beer of Britain (Hobsons Mild).

Variety and diversity are hallmarks of British beers, from gorgeous golden ales to the darkest treacle-like stouts, from light-bodied and low-alcohol ales to great full-bodied whoppers.

Czech Republic

First brewed in Pilsen in the Czech Republic, as we have seen, Pilsner lager is the pale, light, easy-drinking beer that most countries now copy and brew locally. Around 90 per cent of beer consumed in the world is a version of the Czech original, although most of it is a moderate echo of the real thing. To drink pale lager as it should be means a visit to the home of Pilsner.

Dark lagers are also brewed in the Czech Republic and on first sight resemble stout. The coffee and roasted character of stout is there but the body is light, typical of the lager style of beer.

Germany

Germany, one of the world's leading beer cultures, is home to a diverse range of ale and lager styles that have inspired overseas brewers, particularly in the USA, to produce their own versions.

When I die and go to beer heaven, one wing of my local will be dedicated to German beers and I will drink them in a *Biergarten*, with an oompah band playing in the background. I will alternate between wearing a dirndl and lederhosen – essential items in the wardrobes of German beer drinkers. Back on earth, Munich beer gardens are a wonder of the beer world – expansive green oases under leafy linden trees that shade drinkers as they tuck into delicacies such as *Steckerlfisch* (grilled fish-fillet-on-a-stick), *Brezen* (giant doughy pretzels), *Obatzda* (aged Camembert cheese mixed with butter and paprika) and *Bratwurst*, all washed down with steins of foaming beer.

Germans are usually number two in the list of beer consumption per head of population (Czech Republic is number one) and beer is central to their culture. And what a choice they have: pale, crisp, carbonated Helles, one of the most refreshing styles of beer brewed anywhere; the moreish nutty Dunkels; extraordinary pale and dark aromatic Weizen; and a meal in a glass, the spectacular Salvator Doppelbock with the aroma and flavour of dried fruit and sweet caramel, laden with malty goodness.

Nineteenth-century German brewers had a huge impact in the countries they emigrated to. Thank Deutschland for American brands such as Coors, Budweiser and Miller, and for the love affair that Mexicans have with Pilsner, Vienna and dark lagers. Chinese drinkers were introduced to Pilsner in 1903 when an Anglo-German consortium founded Tsingtao brewery. That brand is now the second-biggest selling beer in China.

And, of course, Germans have Oktoberfest in Munich. Could any beer lover resist a nation that lays on one of the greatest parties in the world, when throughout a sixteen-day period more than six million people visit the city to celebrate the art of the brewer?

The festival opens with a twelve-gun salute, after which the mayor ceremoniously opens the first keg of Oktoberfest beer and announces 'O'zapft is!' ('It's tapped!') Only then can people get down to business. During the festival approximately seven million litres of beer are served and some people end up as 'Bierleichen' (beer corpses) – though no doubt they return the following year.

The Netherlands
Although the Netherlands does not produce an indigenous beer style, the local brewers embraced the Pilsner style and produce a number of brands that are amongst the most recognisable beers in the world – Heineken, Amstel and Grolsch.

USA
USA – big country, big beers. That is, if you consider the beers of the increasing number of independent craft brewers. America has only one home-grown type of beer, steam beer – aka California Common – but what US brewers excel at is taking their favourite styles from elsewhere and putting an American spin on them with bigger hops, more alcohol, and an 'anything goes' attitude to brewing. Increasingly, the terms 'extra', 'double' and 'imperial' are used to describe the bolder brews – Flying Dog's Gonzo Imperial Porter and Odell's Myrcenary Double IPA are two superb examples. Some American brewers also create hybrids that do not fit easily into any style of beer – lovable mutts rather than any recognisable pedigree pooch.

Britain's current golden age of brewing, with more than a thousand breweries and new ones opening almost every week, would not have happened without the American craft beer revolution. 'Hail to the Chief.'

Boozers in Britain – the Early Days

Beer is the most sociable of drinks. That's why throughout history the world's great brewing cultures formally established venues for people to meet in and drink beer. The Mesopotamians and Ancient Egyptians had temples and bars, Vikings and Saxons had beer halls, Germany has its beer gardens, and Britain has the pub.

Imagine if the pub had never been invented – where would Britons go to meet their mates, gossip, put the world to rights, flirt and meet prospective lovers, celebrate, commiserate, shelter from the weather? And where would residents of Albert Square and Coronation Street go for a barney?

A pub is more than just a destination for a pint and pickled egg – in Britain it is at the heart of the community and performs an important role as a neutral venue where people can come together, regardless of generation, class, colour, creed, political outlook and sexuality, and socialise together if they want to. What is it about the pub that breaks down the barriers and inhibitions Britons normally have, in a way that cocktail and wine bars do not do? It is a number of factors, starting with the manner of customer service. To buy a drink in a British pub means approaching the bar, bantering with the staff and quite often some other drinkers. There is no table service so that means most people stand up to drink, are more likely to circulate rather than sit in a clique, and can interact with other customers. This creates a casual and buzzing atmosphere. Then there is the beer itself. It is the most egalitarian of all alcoholic drinks and that makes it possible to speak in friendly terms to strangers without being considered suspect.

Hallelujah for the pub! Other countries may have establishments to go and drink beer in but there is nothing like the British boozer, and that is why a visit to a pub is in the top five things that visitors to these shores want to do.

The birth of what we would recognise today as a pub was in the medieval era, when alehouses and inns were established. But Britons had gathered for communal drinking long before then. During the Roman occupation people could visit *tabernae* (from where the word 'tavern' derives) to buy wine, ale and food along major highways. After the Romans had gone, Saxons and Vikings drank beer, cider and mead in halls. Each village had one as the focal point of the community where decisions were made, scores settled, parties hosted and villagers bonded with each other.

Drinking ale was often a matter of life or death in areas where the water could not be trusted. Tea and coffee would not be introduced to Britain until the seventeenth century, so the options of something to drink were limited. Ale provided water, nutrition and, of course, fun. It was a staple of life and was brewed in many homes by women using cooking implements. It cost money to buy malt, and plenty of fuel was required for boiling the wort, so people who could not afford to brew ale at home could go to the local alewife's house and buy a mug or two of ale. They might sit on a bench in a corner of the kitchen, or in a dedicated side room, as the rest of the family went about their business. This is where the term pub comes from – a public house – and even today, most licensees live above the pub.

As more people travelled on pilgrimages to holy sites such as Canterbury Cathedral, monasteries and abbeys became overwhelmed by the Christian duty to provide refreshment and shelter to travellers. Cue the creation of inns offering ale, food and bed, as well as stabling for horses and carriages.

The Black Death plague of 1348 had the unforeseen consequences of increasing demand for ale. This is because the working class people who had survived could ask for higher wages in exchange for their labour, meaning that for the first time they had disposable income to spend on ale. More alehouses were needed to meet demand: the nascent pub had arrived and there was no going back. Not everyone was happy about this, though – especially the ruling classes, who feared that groups of the great unwashed would undoubtedly be plotting insurrection. The king, meanwhile, in the absence of a standing army, depended on ordinary men spending hours practising their longbow skills. In an effort to force men back to the archery butts, pub games were banned in 1366 by Edward III. This may have slowed down the sale of playing cards, but it did not stop people drinking together. By the end of the sixteenth century, England had a population of around four million and just under twenty thousand licensed premises – a very generous one pub for every two hundred people. Compare that with today's one pub per 1,200 people.

Even into the seventeenth century alehouses were considered by the elite to be breeding grounds for antisocial behaviour, where order broke down, treasonous plots were fomented, petty criminals flouted the law, lax morals were tolerated, and the masses wasted their time having fun instead of toiling at work. Successive monarchs and Oliver Cromwell went so far as to suppress alehouses and the activities that happened within their walls. A senior official in the administration of King Charles I said: 'I account alehouses and tippling houses the greatest pests in the kingdom.' Punishments such as fines, public floggings or a few hours in the stocks were levied for public drunkenness. But to no avail – an Englishman's pub was his castle and if he wanted to drink to his heart's content he would. Take it away and who knows what revolutionary sparks might be ignited?

Until the government decided that paving the highways would be good for trade, roads were potholed muddy quagmires that made travel a misery. In 1663 the Turnpikes Act made major highways relatively passable and a network of stagecoach routes encouraged more travel. Merchants, lawyers, tradesmen, people visiting family members or exploring the country took to the road, and this led to the establishment of coaching inns in the centre of towns. Heavy stagecoaches were hauled by six to eight horses that regularly needed resting or replacing; 'hostler' was the term used to describe a stable boy or groom, and this is where the word 'hostelry' derives.

Like the medieval inns for pilgrims, these businesses offered travellers food, drink, accommodation, stabling for horses and farrier services. With the coming of the railways in the nineteenth century, however, the inns that had depended on custom conveyed by horse-drawn carriages lost their primary purpose and had to rely largely on local trade. Only a few survive as pubs/hotels in Britain's towns and cities. The New Inn, Gloucester and the George Inn, Southwark, London are both especially fine.

As late as 1787 the government had seen pubs as dens of immoral behaviour and issued a Royal Proclamation Against Vice, which banned cockfighting, gambling, singing and dancing in alehouses. Even innocent pleasures such as darts and shove ha'penny were suspect because, in the context of drinking, this led to gaming and goodness knows what other nefarious goings-on, according to the suspicious minds of politicians. But it was not beer that was the problem at that time, it was gin. Such was the frenzy for 'mother's ruin' in Britain's major cities, particularly London, that by the middle of the eighteenth century consumption was estimated to be 14 gallons per year for each adult male. Something had to be done about the devastating effect of gin. And the answer was that most benign of wholesome libations – beer. In 1830 the government passed the Beer House Act. This abolished duty on beer and permitted any householder to purchase a licence to open an alehouse. Open season for beer drinkers!

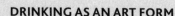

DRINKING AS AN ART FORM

Beer Street, the etching by London artist William Hogarth, is perhaps the greatest visual representation of the wholesomeness of beer. Hogarth was a social commentator and his works reflected the society he knew. *Beer Street* was published in 1751 as a companion piece to *Gin Lane*, which depicts the utter devastation wrought by the eighteenth-century gin frenzy, when countless people (mainly the poor) were permanently sozzled and their lives blighted by excessive consumption of strong spirit. In *Gin Lane*, death stalks the filthy thoroughfares, and characters exist in hopelessness and degradation. Contrast that with *Beer Street*, where happy, healthy, industrious and successful people drink tankards of ale with smiles on their faces.

If the government's idea was to reduce drunkenness, it did not work; people were still inebriated, albeit in a much gentler way than with the deathly lure of gin. A well-known commentator of the era, Sydney Smith, wrote: 'The new beer bill has begun its operations. Everybody is drunk. Those who are not singing are sprawling. The sovereign people are in a beastly state.'

This attempt at social engineering left its mark on the urban landscape, because most existing city pubs date from the years after the Beer House Act came into force. It also inspired the grandest of all pub styles – the gin palace. These were pubs with palatial multi-roomed interiors where no expense was spared on mirrors, carved woodwork, tile work and mosaics. The original owners of these stunning edifices did not build them for the sake of aesthetics; it was all about attracting customers away from competitor pubs by offering the usually poor patrons a few minutes of luxury for the price of a drink.

British pubs have seen many styles throughout the centuries, from the basic, pared-down alehouses to the solid and functional taverns, comfortable coaching inns with horse brasses a-go-go, grand gin palaces and modest corner boozers. All types are still open for business for people to enjoy – Britain's sociable history lives on.

Pubs have always been a community asset and, as such, have played a variety of roles. They have been used as pawnbrokers, prisons, mortuaries, coroner's courts and job centres, when people available for work would gather hoping to be hired by employers; recruiters for the army and navy would find willing men and even press-gang unwilling ones to join up in the pub. Many popular sports developed in or adjacent to the pub on open land – skittles, cricket and bowls. Some of Britain's artists, essayists and literary superstars were avid pub-goers – Chaucer, Hogarth, Shakespeare, Dr Johnson, Dickens and Orwell – inspiration no doubt hitting them over a pint or two. At the end of the nineteenth century social reformer Charles Booth wrote a study of life in London for poor people and concluded that 'Public houses play a larger part in the lives of the people than clubs or friendly societies, churches or missions, or perhaps than all put together'.

Today, as well as being the social nexus of the community, some pubs offer post office services, act as village shops, libraries, Internet cafes and even host school lunch for local children. Centuries after the first British boozer was opened, in countless towns and villages the pub is still undoubtedly the hub!

BEER IS FOR BRUTES

One of England's prize curmudgeons was Philip Stubbes, a sixteenth-century pamphleteer who attacked almost all amusements and contemporary customs in his essays. His best-known work is *The Anatomie of Abuses* (1583) where, in addition to criticising football as 'a bloody and murdering game, not fit for the Sabbath or any other day', and cursing women for wearing 'doublets and jerkins like men's', he reserved special reproach for drunks:

'Every county, city, town, village, and other places hath abundance of alehouses, taverns, and inns, which are so fraught with maltworms night and day that you would wonder to see them. You shall have them there sitting at the wine and good ale all the day long, yea, and night too, peradventure a whole week together so long as any money is left; swilling, gulling and carousing from one to another till never a one can speak a ready word... And a man once drunk with wine or strong drink rather resembling a brute than a Christian man, for do not his eyes begin to stare and be red, fiery and bleared, blubbering forth seas of tears? Doth he not froth and foam at the mouth like a bear? Does not his tongue falter and stammer in his mouth?'

HAVING A QUIET BEER

Unlicensed premises, known generically as 'hush shops', were common in cities in the nineteenth century and some had specific types of clientele. 'Dram shops' were for gin drinkers, while 'flash houses' catered to prostitutes and thieves.

The Knowledge – Beer Trivia

Being taken down a peg or two

Tenth-century Saxon king Edgar was just one of many monarchs and politicians who tried unsuccessfully to curb the beer-drinking habits of his fellow Englishmen. He decreed that communal drinking horns and pottles (wooden vessels) were to be marked with notches or pegs. Drinkers were allowed to sup their share of beer between the pegs, but all this did was encourage people to engage in drinking bouts by 'downing a peg' of beer. Or if someone had drunk more than their share, the others in the group might be angry and, to try and make the remaining beer shares more even, the peg would be moved down to another hole. The term 'taken down a peg or two', as in deflating a person's high opinion of themselves, is believed to derive from this practice of measuring portions of beer.

Last of the alewives

The Black Death plague in Europe (which peaked in 1348–1350) led to the demise of women, or 'alewives', as the primary brewers in England. They had brewed beer at home on a small scale but increased demand following the plague (see 'Boozers in Britain – the Early Days'), especially during wartime, was hard to meet. England was always squaring up to some foreign enemy or other, usually France or Scotland, and soldiers received eight pints of ale a day as their ration – this kept their morale high, and also nourished them. A reliable supply was necessary and could not be provided by domestic brewers. Large-scale brewing by men in commercial breweries became the norm, and women were slowly edged out.

The hip hop

Nowadays, ale and beer are interchangeable terms in Britain but it was not always so. Ale was made with malted barley and might be flavoured with herbs and spices but no hops, therefore it had a sweet base, while beer was also a malted barley drink, but with added hops that gave it a refreshing bitterness. Ale was the hale and hearty drink for good honest English folk, while beer was something to be suspicious of because foreigners in continental Europe drank it. Rumours even spread that hops were harmful. This xenophobic attitude ignored the fact that hops were a natural preservative with antibacterial properties that gave beer a longer shelf life than ale, which soured in a couple of days.

The first record of hopped beer in Blighty was when it was imported from Amsterdam into Great Yarmouth in about 1362. Local brewers were not impressed enough to try brewing it themselves, and the earliest mention of beer being brewed in England (from imported hops) was in 1412, when a German alewife in Colchester made it. Cultivation of hops most probably did not begin until around 1520, when *Humulus lupulus* was planted in Kent. But centuries of ale-drinking by Englishmen and women was not to be abandoned easily, and ale and beer continued to be brewed and consumed as distinctly different beverages. King Henry VIII's brewer produced ale and beer for the royal household and Henry's army marched on hopped beer.

Supplies did not always reach the soldiers overseas in time, as evidenced by one army commander who wrote to complain that his forces had consumed no beer for ten days, 'which is strange for English men to do with so little grudging'.

No one knows exactly when traditional unhopped ale ceased being popular – possibly in the eighteenth century – in favour of the hopped beer that came to dominate brewing. It is also not clear when hopped beer started to be referred to as 'ale'.

A different kind of brew

Consumption of beer decreased in Britain in the mid to late nineteenth century as clean water became easier to source and the tax on tea was cut, which meant that tea was no longer a luxury only the wealthy could afford. Tea became the everyday drink for the masses at the expense of beer.

What's in a name?

Where do the names of two of Britain's most popular beers originate?

Kent brewery Shepherd Neame's Bishop's Finger is named after the wooden signposts that directed pilgrims along the route to the shrine of St Thomas à Becket in Canterbury Cathedral before it was destroyed during the Dissolution of the Monasteries in the late 1530s. Most people were illiterate in the medieval era but, even if they were unable to read the word 'Canterbury', they could recognise the wooden finger pointing them in the right direction.

Fuller's London Pride is named after a garden flower (*Saxifraga x urbium*) that was often found growing in bomb craters in the capital during World War Two.

Where's the party?

In medieval Britain, anything was an excuse for a party. Celebrations were known as 'ales' and special beers were brewed to mark major milestones in life, such as the 'Child Ale' (birth of a baby); the 'Christening Ale' (baptism); the 'Bride Ale' (wedding) and the 'Give Ale' (funeral), where the beer was paid for by the deceased so his or her friends could ease the ensuing journey into the afterlife with cheers and good wishes.

Churches would also arrange ales ('Church Ales'). These were fund-raisers, following which the money collected by the sale of ale to partygoers went into church coffers or was distributed to the poor. All other brewing was temporarily banned and the only source of ale to be purchased was that commissioned by the parish. Parishioners were also expected to pay for the brewing ingredients. These festivities were compulsory and so less popular than ad hoc shindigs.

'Bede Ales' on the other hand were exceedingly popular – especially with the needy. If a person had fallen on hard times through no fault of their own, their friends were allowed by the parish to hold a party and proceeds from the sale of beer were donated to the pauper to help change their fortunes.

Getting off scot-free

When a person gets off scot-free it means they have escaped punishment or benefitted from something without paying for it. The phrase dates back to medieval England and the 'scot' (the word derives from the Norse *skat*, meaning 'tax') was levied by the church on each parishioner to pay for beer brewed for Church Ales. Villagers took to gathering for parties in the forest outside the jurisdiction of common law, where they drank their ale 'scot-free'.

This skullduggery enraged church authorities and they appealed to the all-powerful bishops to ban 'Scot Ales' – with little success.

Meet Sir John

Sir John Barleycorn is the fictitious personification of barley, and poems and drinking songs described the indignities he suffered to make the national drink. Sir John came to represent the sturdy character of rural English people; the song below is a traditional one:

(Spoken)
There were three men, Came from the west
Their fortunes for to tell and the life of John Barleycorn as well.

(Sung)
They laid him in three furrows deep,
Laid clods upon his head,
Then these three men made a solemn vow
John Barleycorn was dead.

Chorus:
Fa-la La-la it's a lucky day!
Sing Fa-la La-a-lay-o
Fa-la La-la, it's a lucky day!
Singin' Fa-la La-la lay-o

They let him die for a very long time
Till the rain from heaven did fall,
Then little Sir John sprang up his head
And he did amaze them all. (Chorus)

They let him stand till the midsummer day,
Till he looked both pale and wan.

The little Sir John he grew a long beard
And so became a man. (Chorus)

They have hired men with the scythes so sharp,
To cut him off at the knee,
They rolled him and they tied him around the waist,
They served him barbarously. (Chorus)

They have hired men with the crab-tree sticks,
To cut him skin from bone,
And the miller has served him worse than that,
For he's ground him between two stones. (Chorus)

They've wheeled him here, they've wheeled him there,
They've wheeled him to a barn,
And they have served him worse than that,
They've bunged him in a vat. (Chorus)

They have worked their will on John Barleycorn
But he lived to tell the tale,
For they pour him out of an old brown jug
And they call him home brewed ale. (Chorus)

Fancy a quarter?

Magna Carta, or The Great Charter of the Liberties of England, proved how important ale was in medieval Albion because Clause 35 stated: 'There shall be standard measures of wine, ale, and corn throughout the kingdom.' The measure was called a London quarter, or two pints. Woe betide anyone who served short – they could be fined or strapped into a ducking stool as punishment. The law was superseded by the Sheriff's Act of

1887. Nowadays legal measures for beer in a pub are a third, a half, and one pint.

Situation vacant

How about a job as the parish 'Sin Eater'? All that is required is to eat some bread washed down with ale and soak up a few sins. Sin eaters (often beggars) were paid to stand over the corpse of someone who had died suddenly without confessing their transgressions. The idea was that by consuming the food and drink, a sin eater ingested the deceased's sins, thereby permitting the soul to reach heaven. This tradition was widespread on the Wales–England border until the nineteenth century.

The good life

Have you heard the term 'cakes and ale', referring to pleasure and all that is good in life? Shakespeare's character Sir Toby Belch mentions it in a conversation with Malvolio in *Twelfth Night*: 'Dost thou think, because thou art virtuous, there shall be no more cakes and ale?' But the Bard did not invent the phrase because a translation of an Ancient Egyptian 'Book of the Dead', written around 1240 BC, includes it in the following passage:

But let the state of the spirits be given unto me instead of water and air, and the satisfying of the longings of love, and let the quietness of heart be given unto me instead of cakes and ale.

Plea for the pub

Hilaire Belloc (1870–1953), French-born poet, historian and essayist, was an Anglophile extraordinaire who settled in Sussex and became a British citizen. Going to the pub should be mandatory for Britons and Belloc was an enthusiast.

Best known for his *Cautionary Tales for Children*, he also wrote in earnest when he issued a plea for Britons to cherish the pub and to resist the tide of closures. It ended with the warning: 'But when you have lost your Inns drown your empty selves, for you will have lost the last of England.'

Each time a pub closes in Britain, the ghost of that French champion of the boozer stirs and whispers his prescient warning.

Hopping down to Kent

Today hops are machine-harvested, but until the 1960s they were picked by hand by seasonal workers who often came from big cities into the countryside. In Britain one of the major hop-growing regions was Kent and this led to a phenomenon known as 'Hopping down to Kent', when each September armies of women and children would descend on farms and stay for six weeks for the hop harvest. These labourers usually came from deprived parts of London and this was an opportunity to escape city pollution and breathe fresh country air. But this was no holiday resort – accommodation was in cramped tin huts, tents or animal shelters, and cooking facilities and, more importantly, sanitation and hygiene were rudimentary at best. The menfolk who worked during the week in London would visit their families at the weekend.

Country folk were suspicious of the urban incomers, treating them all as scoundrels by securing goods in shops behind chicken wire, and segregating pubs with one room for locals and the other, uncarpeted and basic, for the pickers. As they were generally unwelcome in villages, the pickers spent most of their recreational time on the farm singing songs around a campfire – including this 'Hop-picker's anthem':

Now hopping's just beginning,
We've got our time to spend.
We've only come down hopping,
To earn a quid if we can
With a tee-I-ay, tee-I-ay, tee-I-ee-I-ay.

Now early Monday morning,
The measurer he'll come round.
'Pick your hops all ready,
You'll pick them off the ground'
With a tee-I-ay, tee-I-ay, tee-I-ee-I-ay.

Now early Tuesday morning,
The bookie he'll come round
With a bag of money,
He'll flop it on the ground.
Saying, 'Do you want some money?'
'Yes sir if you please,
To buy a hock of bacon
And a roll of mouldy cheese'
With a tee-I-ay, tee-I-ay, tee-I-ee-I-ay.

They say all hopping's lousy,
I believe it's true.
Since I've been down hopping,

I've got a chat or two
With a tee-I-ay, tee-I-ay, tee-I-ee-I-ay.

Early Saturday morning,
It is our washing day.
We'll boil 'em in our hopping pot,
And we hangs 'em o'er the ground
With a tee-I-ay, tee-I-ay, tee-I-ee-I-ay.

I say one, I say two,
No more hopping shall I do
With a tee-I-ay, tee-I-ay, tee-I-ee-I-ay.

Water, water everywhere and not a drop to drink

When the Pilgrim Fathers set sail on the *Mayflower* in 1620 for a new life in the American Colonies they were heading for the mouth of the Hudson river (New York). But supplies of beer and other victuals ran out and they were forced to land in Massachusetts. Alas, there was no beer to be found, which meant they had to risk drinking the local water and it was eight years before a ship, the *Arbella*, landed from Britain with new immigrants and 10,000 gallons of beer.

RIP John Randal

This epitaph worthy of a committed ale drinker adorns a seventeenth-century gravestone in Saint Michael and All Angels Church, Great Wolford, Warwickshire:

HERE old John Randal lies,
Who, counting from his tale,
Liv'd threescore years and ten,

Such vertue was in ale.
Ale was his meat,
Ale was his drink,
Ale did his heart revive,
And if he could have drunk his ale,
He still had been alive. –
He died January 5, 1698.

Fit for a queen

Queen Elizabeth I is one of history's celebrated beer drinkers. For centuries beer was consumed with every meal from breakfast to supper – and for refreshment in between. A household the size of Elizabeth's would require vast supplies so brewers would have been employed to provide it. When she travelled on one of her annual Royal Progresses, so did her court, and this consisted of over a thousand people, all of whom needed feeding and watering.

Robert Dudley, Earl of Leicester – the queen's favourite – was responsible for court ceremonial and in charge of the organisation of festivities, including ensuring the booze was up to scratch. During a progress to Hatfield House in Hertfordshire, he wrote to Elizabeth's chief adviser Sir William Cecil and complained 'there was not one drop of good drink for her there. We were fain to send to London and Kenilworth and divers other places where ale was; her own bere (sic) was so strong as there was no man able to drink it.'

Before a visit to Tutbury Castle in Staffordshire, courtier Sir Francis Walsingham wrote to the castle governor and asked, 'What place neere Tutbury beere may be provided for Her Majestie's use?' The reply was, 'At Burton, three myles off.'

Mary, Queen of Scots was keen on the ale brewed by monks at Burton Abbey (the same town that later became a brewing powerhouse) and had it delivered to her during her long captivity in Fotheringay Castle near Peterborough until her execution in 1587.

The A-list

Throughout history more people have consumed beer than have not. With beer being such a staple, it means that almost all the best-known personalities of the past were beer drinkers. They include Cleopatra, Queen of the Nile. She would have had her own brewers to supply the royal household. Tutankhamun, Egypt's boy king, did not just drink beer in life, but also in the afterlife, as jars of beer were discovered in his tomb. Literary icon Jane Austen (who lived 1775–1817) enjoyed a drink, as evidenced in her letters, and she was also a home brewer. Spruce beer was one of her specialities – made with the needles and buds of the tree, and treacle and ginger for flavouring. Spruce beer was also carried on Captain Cook's ship, the *Endeavour*, as he explored the Pacific Ocean. Spruce is high in vitamin C and was consumed to prevent scurvy amongst the crew. Arguably the highest-profile beer drinker in the world today is US president Barack Obama, who is often photographed with a full glass in his hand. He is so keen that he bought a home-brew kit and the White House chef has been brewing beer and adding honey from hives in the White House garden.

Dearly beer-loved

The word 'bride' is thought to derive from the Old English 'bryd', itself believed to originate from a Germanic root 'bru', meaning to cook or brew. In medieval England the parents of a betrothed couple would collect money from villagers to pay for the ingredients to make a special brew for the wedding reception, aka the 'Bride Ale'. Over time this term was corrupted to the word 'bridal'. Guests were required to purchase their drinks by donating cash to the newly-weds for use in setting up house. Today guests buy wedding gifts from John Lewis instead, and may get a glass or two of Chardonnay in return, but the purpose is still the same.

Davy Jones' ale

When prime minister Winston Churchill discovered during World War Two that armed forces stationed in the Far East were rationed to three bottles of beer a month, he insisted something be done to increase the supply. The ingenious remedy was to assemble a brewing kit on a naval amenity ship called *MV Menestheus*. Distilled seawater, malt, hop extract and yeast produced a brew called 'Davy Jones' Ale' on the world's only floating brewery.

Barmy about beer

'Barm' is another word for the yeast that froths on beer and other fermented drinks. In parts of northern England, especially in Lancashire, it is used to make bread rolls known as barm cakes. Barm is also the origin of the term 'barmy', used to describe someone who is 'bonkers' or frothing at the mouth.

For the chop

Today's beer-tax evaders may get a virtual slap on the wrist but for thirteenth-century residents of the French city of Aix-la-Chapelle the punishment was more severe. Their right hand was chopped off, they were banished for five years, and the house or building in which the beer was brewed or sold was demolished.

Gone for a Burton

'Burton snatch' is a term that might sound rather vulgar (wash your ears out!) but it does in fact refer to the quick hint of sulphur aroma on some pale ales. This phenomenon is caused by calcium sulphate in the water and is especially noticeable on beers such as Marston's Pedigree brewed in Burton-upon-Trent. Burton's historic dominance as a brewing centre of pale ale was due to the mineral content of the local water – high in calcium sulphate and therefore the perfect water for brewing pale ale. It extracts less colour from the malt, meaning that ultra-pale beers can be produced; it enhances the flavours in the malts and the hop oils; and it imparts a dry crisp mouthfeel, which is characteristic of the style. Brewers not fortunate enough to be in areas with that type of water can add mineral salts to achieve the same effect and this process is known as 'Burtonising' the water.

Before Burton became celebrated for pale ale, a brown, sweet but highly hopped beer known simply as 'Burton ale' was the superstar from the East Midlands. This was no parochial brew, however, because international clients in Russia and the Baltic states clamoured for it. By the late eighteenth and early nineteenth centuries, around 70 per cent of annual production of Burton ale was sent down the River Trent to Hull for onward export to the Baltic region. This trade came to an end for two reasons – the Russians began to levy tariffs on English imports, and during the Napoleonic Wars 'Boney's' navy blockaded the required sea routes.

Those Burton brewers, such as William Worthington and Samuel Allsopp, were resourceful men and, rather than rue the fact that their beers could not reach the market in the north, they looked east and noticed that London brewer George Hodgson had a lucrative trade exporting pale ale to India. In 1822 Allsopp experimented and discovered that the water in Burton made much better pale ale than London water did. The local water was the saviour of the Burton brewers and within ten years half the beer brewed in the town was exported to India.

King of beer

Jan Gambrinus, the mythical King of Beer, is often depicted in ermine, wearing a crown, holding a mug of ale and riding a giant cask. His birthday, celebrated on 11 April, is a good excuse to raise a glass. According to the fable, King Gambrinus was bestowed with the gift of beer by Isis, the Egyptian goddess of fertility. His legend may have been inspired by two real men – Jan Primus, Duke of Brabant (in what is now Belgium), who lived in the late thirteenth century and played a senior role in the Brussels Brewing Guild; and Jean sans Peur aka John the Fearless (1371–1419), Duke of Burgundy, who had an erroneous reputation as the person who invented hopped beer.

Patron saints of beer

While Sumerians and Babylonians celebrated their beer deities, the Christian church's holy beer benefactors are patron saints. Quite often these are monks canonised for the miracles they performed – some of which involved the magical multiplication of beer, similar to the biblical story of Jesus and the loaves and fishes.

One familiar name is Saint Wenceslas, tenth-century king of Czechoslovakia, who championed the spread of Christianity in his home nation. Having allegedly protected highly valued Bohemian hops by threatening capital punishment for anyone who exported them from the country, he is the patron saint of Czech brewers.

Patron saint of Belgian brewers and hop-pickers is Arnold of Soissons, who lived in the mid eleventh century. He was abbot of a local monastery and when beer supplies ran low he asked God to send more. His prayers were answered and miraculously the cupboard was replenished.

Saint Arnold (also known as Arnulf) was a seventh-century bishop of Metz, who warned people not to drink polluted water but instead to consume beer as a safer alternative. He is reputed to have said, 'From man's sweat and God's love, beer came into the world.'

Historic alternatives to hops

When there was a shortage of hops in previous centuries, or when the price of hops was high, brewers used a variety of flowers, seeds, leaves and twigs with bitter qualities as alternatives. In 1710 the British government passed a law to prohibit the use of any bittering agent other than hops in beer. This was a money-spinner rather than an incentive for brewers to make wholesome beer because duty was levied on hops. But some brewers ignored the ruling and continued to spice up their brews with various other substances. Some of these had an intoxicating effect, which meant brewers would save money because they could use less of the expensive malt as the source of sugar to ferment into alcohol, but drinkers still got the required buzz. A skull-and-crossbones warning should have been stamped on beer barrels because a number of the additives were poisonous in large amounts. Beer drinkers often took their lives in their glass when they unwittingly consumed any of the following in large enough quantities:

Belladonna (aka deadly nightshade): bitter with intoxicating effects, it contains the toxic alkaloid atropine.

Bitter bean: used for bitterness, it contains strychnine.

Bearded darnel: has intoxicating effects. Is also narcotic and can cause blindness.

Chaste tree: used for bitterness but, as the name suggests, it diminishes libido.

Common clary: has intoxicating effects and is also narcotic.

Colocynth: occasionally used for bittering but is a violent and poisonous purgative (of the stomach).

Foxglove (aka digitalis): used for its bitterness and intoxicating properties. It is poisonous, purgative (especially of the bowels), produces giddiness and can kill.

Henbane: used for bitterness and to make beer more intoxicating. It contains the poisonous alkaloids scopolamine and hyoscyamine, can cause nausea, delirium and vomiting, and can kill.

Nux vomica: used for bitterness, it contains the poisonous alkaloids strychnine and brucine.

White poppy: used to make beer more intoxicating, it is also narcotic.

Wormwood: used for bitterness. In high doses it is addictive and poisonous. In the eighteenth century a physician commented on the use of wormwood in beer, saying: 'does not only hurt, but by degrees weakens the natural heat of the stomach and sends heavy dull vapours to the head and so prejudiceth the eyes.'

Yarrow: used for bitterness and to make beer more intoxicating. In excess it can cause dizziness and ringing in the ears.

Yew: used to make beer more intoxicating. In large doses it is poisonous.

Birra Italiana

Italy may have the lowest consumption of beer per head in Europe and a limited culture of brewing, but that has not stopped a growing number of inventive brewers freeing their imagination and experimenting with exotic ingredients such as myrrh, roses, pomegranate, gentian root and clams to create some ingenious brews. Birra Baladin is one of the leaders of the Italian beery innovation, producing big-flavoured beers, many of them aged for months in old rum, wine and whisky casks.

Swotting for the Pub Quiz – Frequently Asked Questions and More

Some of these subjects may be covered elsewhere in the book but they are the questions I am most often asked, so here they are together for easy reference. There are also some more obscure facts that are handy for answering the trickier pub quiz questions!

When and where was beer first brewed?

No one knows when or where beer was first brewed. The most likely scenario is that humans in different parts of the world noticed that something magical happened to damp rice or barley grains when microscopic airborne yeast fermented the cereal sugars. So far the earliest evidence of a fermented cereal beverage (made from rice) is at an archaeological site in China's Henan province dating back to around 7000 BC. That does not mean beer was first brewed 9,000 years ago, however, it just means that earlier proof has not yet been discovered. Ancient societies in Africa, the Amazon region, the Middle East and China had independent knowledge of beer so the most accurate answer available as to when and where beer was first brewed is: 'Ages ago and anywhere that cereal grew.'

What causes the head on beer?

The foam on top of beer is a reaction between protein in malt, compounds in hops, and carbon dioxide bubbles. Drinkers in different parts of Britain prefer a certain type of head. In Yorkshire and other parts of the north, beer without a big tight creamy head is not beer; whereas in London and parts of the south-east, where little to no head is the norm, a beer with such a substantial head may spur the comment, 'If I had wanted ice cream, I would have asked for it.' Head size and consistency is influenced by the method of dispensing beer from a handpump or tap. Some pubs serve cask ale through curved spouts called 'swan necks', which reach all the way inside the glass to the base so the beer is filled from bottom to top, creating foam. In the absence of a swan neck, bar staff can add an implement called a sparkler to the nozzle where beer is forced through small holes – this can be loosened or tightened to give the required head.

Where did the name 'India pale ale' (IPA) originate?

There is a lot of rubbish on the Internet, and some of it relates to the provenance of India pale ale. The oft-repeated myth is that the beer was invented for British soldiers in India and was especially hoppy and strong to survive a long sea journey to the subcontinent. It's true that a highly hopped strong beer would mature beautifully during the long voyage east and arrive at its destination in peak condition, but the beer was not invented for the Indian market. It was not even called India pale ale until decades after it had first been exported from London. The beer style already existed and was called 'October ale', referred to in a 1768 pamphlet as 'October malt wine' – a high-alcohol, heavily hopped pale beer intended for long maturation. A brewer named George Hodgson of the Bow Brewery in east London, near to the docks where ships trading with India were berthed, created his own version of the October beer.

189

Ship captains purchased it as victuals for the crew and also to sell to traders at their destination, so October ale found its way to India and became enormously popular. Hodgson soon had a lucrative trade and other brewers, based in Burton-upon-Trent, wanted a share, so they started to brew a similar style of beer and sell it at a lower price. They also rebranded the beer and by around 1829 it was being sold as India pale ale.

What does top- and bottom-fermenting beer mean?

These terms are shorthand for explaining what branch of the family tree a beer belongs in, and refer to what happens to yeast after it has fermented the beer. With ale, most of the yeast spores gather and rise to the surface of the beer as a creamy foam. Lager yeast acts in a different way because the spores sink to the bottom of the fermenting vessel. So ale is top-fermenting and lager is bottom-fermenting. This definition is not truly accurate, though, because some yeast spores are unpredictable and do what they want – some rising to the top and others going to the bottom of the fermenting vessel. However, describing them as top- or bottom-fermenting is an easy-to-understand way of classifying beer styles as ale or lager.

Why is draught Guinness so creamy and the bottled beer not?

That gorgeous, thick, creamy head on draught Guinness comes from a process called 'smooth flow', also known as 'cream flow' or 'nitrokeg'. A mixture of nitrogen and carbon dioxide (usually a ratio of 75/25) is mixed into the beer to give that ultra-smooth mouthfeel. The bottles and cans contain a gadget called a widget that releases the gas blend as the beer is poured, but not in the amount that the draught beer has.

What is the difference between pale ale and India pale ale?

An authentic India pale ale should be highly hopped, aromatic and 5% ABV and above. Usually the hop character is more dominant than that of the malt. When India pale ale became a major success as an export beer in the early nineteenth century, British brewers started to produce a domestic version for sale in pubs. It was known as 'pale ale', which earned the nickname 'bitter' to differentiate it from sweeter beers on the bar, i.e. mild and porter. Just to confuse the issue, Greene King and Deuchars brew beers called IPA (shorthand for India pale ale) but neither of those brands have the big hop character that is typical of the style.

What is the difference between ale and lager?

Both ale and lager are beers made from water, malt, hops and yeast. Think of Darjeeling, Assam, Earl Grey, Oolong and green – all teas, just different versions; it is the same with different branches of the beer family – ales form one and lager another (Lambic is a third branch, a speciality Belgian style of beer). Under the 'ale' banner come mild, pale ale, India pale ale, Weizen, porter, stout, Trappist, oud bruin and dozens of other styles. With lager there is Pilsner, Vienna, amber, Dunkel, Bock, Helles and many others.

The water used for brewing lager is light in mineral salts, whereas with ale it is the opposite. The brewing process is the same for lager and ale, but what happens during fermentation differs. Ale is fermented with warm-fermenting yeast that contributes aroma and flavour to the beer during a swift fermentation. For lager, the brewer uses cool-fermenting yeast that ferments slowly and gives little aroma. Authentic lager (as opposed to the mass-produced commercial brands that are hurriedly produced) is left to mature for several weeks, even months, in cool conditions and this develops clean and uncomplicated flavours and a smooth character.

After maturation most lager is pasteurised and carbonated, but not always. The Scottish brewer Harviestoun brews an excellent pale lager called Schiehallion that is often available as a cask-conditioned beer, served in a pub the way real ale is through a hand-pull, i.e. unpasteurised. To some people, lager is a dirty word that means pale, fizzy, bland beer. That is because many major brewers around the world create just such a product. Avoid those brewers and instead check out authentic Czech and German Pilsners.

What is the difference between porter and stout?

The styles of beer are similar. Porter is mahogany in colour with coffee and chocolate aroma and flavour, whereas stout is almost black and has distinct charred, treacle, liquorice and chicory characters. Both were invented in London.

Stout originally meant brave or proud before it came to mean 'strong'. It was first recorded in connection with beer around 1630 and was soon common terminology for describing a high-alcohol, full-flavoured brew of any colour, whether pale or dark. Today's drinker would be surprised to be handed a pale stout – but such beers do exist. The Durham Brewery's White Stout is excellent.

So what most people recognise today as stout – a dark coffee-like beer – started off as stout porter. In nineteenth-century Britain, porter was the most widely brewed beer and the strong version was known as brown stout. As pale stout lost popularity, porter brewers claimed the term so eventually it came to refer to dark beer.

What is the difference between cask-conditioned and pasteurised beer?

Cask-conditioned beer is also known as 'real ale' or 'cask ale'. It is unfiltered and unpasteurised and usually dispensed by the action of hand-pumping a handle on the bar so the beer flows through plastic tubes from the cask in the cellar. Any subtle carbonation in the beer is natural and caused by the secondary fermentation it goes through in the cask. This is beer in its most natural state. Yeast is present in the cask although most of it will have sunk to the bottom of the vessel. Cask beer needs to be cared for carefully by the cellar manager to ensure it is in top condition. This means it must be fresh, served at the perfect temperature, and the cellar and all dispense equipment regularly cleaned.

Pasteurised or 'kegged' beer is filtered of yeast and then artificially carbonated with carbon dioxide and nitrogen. It is packaged in a pressurised container – a keg – and when a tap is flipped at the bar gas pressure forces the beer from the keg along plastic tubes into the glass. It is normally served at a lower temperature than cask ale is and often has a fizzy mouthfeel. Compared to cask ale this beer is low maintenance.

Is there any milk in milk stout?

Not whole milk, but this style of beer does contain lactose, aka milk sugar. Yeast does not ferment this sugar so it remains in the finished beer, adding a sweet taste and creamy mouthfeel. Milk stout is also known as 'cream stout' or 'sweet stout'. Mackeson is the best-known brand and it is still brewed, albeit on a small scale. In its glory days it was advertised with the strapline: 'Looks good, tastes good and, by golly, it does you good.'

Is Guinness really good for you?

No more than any other beer. 'Guinness is Good For You' was one of the marketing slogans used in the past by Guinness and it stuck in people's minds. Many believe that, of all beer brands, Guinness has the most goodness. They also think it has more iron than any other (it does not) – and cite the fact that it was recommended for nursing mothers. The power of advertising!

Consumed moderately, all beer made with 100 per cent real ingredients (rather than extracts or flavourings) is wholesome.

What are the different names for beer casks?

Nowadays most pubs sell their beer from a nine-gallon cask called a firkin. But there are smaller and larger sizes of cask.

Pin or polypin: 4.5 gallons or 36 pints

Firkin: 9 gallons or 72 pints

Kilderkin: 18 gallons or 144 pints

Barrel: 36 gallons or 288 pints

Hogshead: 54 gallons or 432 pints

Butt: 108 gallons or 864 pints

Tun: 216 gallons or 1,728 pints

What is 'black and tan'?

Beer blends such as 'black and tan' have now gone out of fashion, but in Britain this habit of mixing a porter or stout with a paler-coloured beer was common from the eighteenth century.

What is 'black velvet'?

Guinness and Champagne, served in a flute. London private members' club Brooks's claims that this cocktail was invented there in 1861 to mourn the death of Queen Victoria's husband, Prince Albert.

What is an 'ale-conner'?

In the medieval era when ale and beer were such essential commodities in England and Europe, there were laws to safeguard the quality of the brew and ensure customers were not being cheated with short measures. In England, officials known as 'ale-conners' (aka 'ale-tasters') were appointed to visit alehouses and check the wares. It sounds like a dream job but they were not permitted to drink too much lest they actually *enjoy* themselves!

There is no contemporary evidence to support the oft-repeated anecdote that ale-conners wore leather britches and would pour ale onto a wooden bench and then sit down in it. After thirty minutes if the leather britches stuck to the bench the beer was (depending on who is telling the story) either bad or good. Another version of the tale suggests that if the ale-conner was stuck to the bench then it meant the beer was high in alcohol (residual sugars in the brew being sticky) and so more duty would be levied.

There are honorary ale-conners today in the City of London and they continue the spurious habit of donning leather trousers and then sitting in pools of beer. A waste of good ale!

How is non-alcoholic beer made?

In America it is called 'near beer'. Many beers marketed as alcohol-free still contain a miniscule amount of alcohol (generally less than

0.5% ABV). These beers are brewed as normal and then the alcohol is removed using one of a number of methods: reverse osmosis, evaporation, vacuum distillation, or by removing yeast after a limited fermentation. These beers usually have a watery body and little flavour and should be retitled 'Don't-go-near beer'.

The Lingo – Glossary of Beer Terms

To be fluent in beer, one must know the language. Here are some common terms used in brewing:

Alcohol by volume (ABV): this is a measure of alcohol strength and is determined by the percentage of alcohol in the total volume of liquid. The brewer uses an instrument called a hydrometer to gauge the density of liquid in relation to water. The denser the liquid, the higher the level of alcohol.

Ale: a diverse selection of styles from one branch of the beer family tree, made with warm-fermenting yeasts. Styles include abbey, India pale ale, stout, Kölsch, porter, mild and many others. Ales are sometimes described as top-fermenting beers – a reference to where the yeast cells usually end up in the fermenting vessel.

Body: body refers to the density of the liquid in the mouth. It is caused by soluble carbohydrates – in beer these come from the malt. Beer is normally described as light, medium or full-bodied. The body of beer and its alcohol content are connected because of sugar carbs in the brew. Higher sugar levels mean a higher potential alcohol content. If sugar levels are low to begin with then the yeast has little to ferment, so alcohol levels will be low.

Bottle-conditioned: beer that undergoes a secondary fermentation in the bottle. This happens either by adding wort or sugar to unfiltered beer to revive the yeast and then sealing the bottle; or by bottling filtered beer and adding a dose of new yeast before the bottle is sealed. After a few weeks the yeast goes dormant and settles at the bottom of the bottle as sediment – that is why bottle-conditioned beers normally have a slight cloudiness. A high-alcohol bottle-conditioned beer will age over the years and change its flavour profile. Some brewers bottle their cask ales but do not add extra wort, sugar or yeast, so technically these are not bottle-conditioned but can be described as real ale in a bottle.

In French the equivalent term to 'bottle-conditioned' is '*sur levure*' or '*sur lie, fermentation en bouteille*'; in Flemish: '*op gist*' or '*hergist in de fles*'; in German: '*mit Hefe*' or '*naturtrüb*'; and in Dutch: '*op gist*' or '*met gist*'.

Bottom fermentation: this refers to lager styles such as Pilsner, Dunkel and Helles. Lager yeast strains normally drop to the bottom of the fermenting vessel. In this book beer styles are classified as warm (top) or cool (bottom) fermenting beers. (See also 'Cool-fermenting yeast'.)

Bright beer: usually refers to beer that has been pasteurised and filtered of yeast and protein particles, so it has great clarity. However, some unfiltered and unpasteurised cask-conditioned (aka real ale) and bottle-conditioned beers are described as bright beer when the yeast sediment and protein has dropped to the bottom of the vessel or bottle.

'Burtonisation' (aka 'Burtonising'): the ideal water for brewing pale ale and bitter is high in calcium sulphate. Burton-upon-Trent water is naturally high in that essential mineral salt and this causes a phenomenon known colloquially as the 'Burton snatch', where beer drinkers may notice a whiff of sulphur for an instant when they take their first drink of a Burton-brewed beer. Brewers in other parts of the world can 'Burtonise' their water by adding calcium sulphate (aka gypsum) salts.

CAMRA: Campaign for Real Ale, founded in England in 1971. The campaigning zeal of CAMRA's members saved British beer from the fate of bland, fizzy, characterless, pasteurised brews. In the 1960s and 1970s many brewers ceased supplying their customers with cask-conditioned ale – it was considered to be old-fashioned, with a flat-cap image that many major beer makers wanted to forget in the brave new world of filtered, chilled, carbonated Pilsner lager. CAMRA worked ceaselessly to protect Britain's unique style of serving beer – live beer hand-pumped from casks through pipes.

Candi sugar: this is caramelised sugar, usually liquid, that a brewer adds for the additional flavours it gives to the beer. It is widely used in Belgian brewing, especially with abbey and Trappist beers. When candi sugar is fully fermented the result is a dry, lightish-bodied beer but with high alcohol content.

Carbonation: all beer is carbonated because carbon dioxide is a by-product of fermentation. With real ale, aka cask-conditioned ale, the CO_2 might not be noticeable because it is dissolved in the beer rather than being visible as bubbles. Pasteurised beer is artificially carbonated with CO_2 and often a mix of nitrogen. The gas will be apparent to the eye and on the palate, adding a spiky and refreshing mouthfeel.

Cask-conditioned ale: a pub that has handpumps on the bar has cask-conditioned ale in its cellar. Also known as 'real ale', this style of dispensing beer is British through and through. The beer is neither pasteurised nor filtered, and the yeast is still live and present in the cask. The publican ensures that the yeast settles to the bottom of the cask so the drinker does not consume it. When served, the beer should be bright and clear, unless it is meant to be cloudy, with a fresh appearance and taste.

Cask Marque: many British pubs have a Cask Marque certificate in the window or a plaque outside on the wall. This is a sign that the beer inside is in excellent condition. Cask Marque is an independent organisation with a team of inspectors who arrive unannounced and check that the pub cellar and beer is maintained to the highest quality. Although the publicans have signed up to the Cask Marque scheme, they do not know when inspection will take place.

Cool-fermenting yeast: brewers of lager-style beer use a strain of yeast that is a hybrid of two species of sugar-loving fungus – *Saccharomyces cerevisiae* and *Saccharomyces bayanus*. It ferments slowly at a cool temperature of 10–15 °C, and it typically ferments more of the sugars in the beer than ale yeast (*Saccharomyces cerevisiae* on its own*)* does, leading to a lighter body and crisper taste. Beers brewed with this strain of yeast are often called 'bottom-fermenting', a reference to where most of the yeast cells end up in the vessels after fermentation. (See also 'Bottom fermentation'.)

Draught beer: beer that is served from a cask or keg rather than a bottle or can.

Dry hopping: brewers who want more hop character in the beer will add hops not just during the boiling phase of brewing, but also to the fermenting vessel, maturation vessel and sometimes even in the cask. Something of a misnomer, as it is more akin to 'steeping' than to 'drying'.

Esters: aromas and flavours produced by the reactions of organic compounds and alcohol during fermentation. They are fruity and sometimes spicy, for example the clove aroma in wheat beer.

Fermentation: the process whereby yeast converts sugars to alcohol, carbon dioxide and heat. Flavours and aromas are also produced – particularly with ale yeast and wild yeast. The word derives from the Latin word *'fevere'* – to boil.

Filtration: pasteurised beer is filtered to remove dead yeast cells, solids such as hops, and protein that causes a haze, all so the beer has clarity. Cask-conditioned real ale is not filtered.

Finings: these are organic compounds used to improve the clarity of beer by removing unwanted solids such as proteins and yeast cells that cause a haze. They work by attracting the solids to stick together so they become heavy enough to sink to the bottom of the vessel. Carageenan (a by-product of algae or seaweed), egg white, gelatin and gum arabic solutions are often used, as well as isinglass. (See also 'What is isinglass?' in the chapter headed 'Do the Brew'.)

Finish: a term used in beer, wine, and cider-tasting to describe how long the flavour lingers after swallowing. In beer-tasting it is sometimes known as the 'hang'.

German Beer Purity Law: see 'Reinheitsgebot'.

Green-hop beer: beer that is brewed with freshly picked hops that have not been dried. Speed is of the essence with green hops because unless they are used in the brew within forty-eight hours of harvesting they may start to rot. Green-hop beer has an intensely fresh hop character.

Grist: this is the term for malted cereal after it has been milled into a rough powder – hence the term 'grist for the mill'. The grist goes into the mash tun and hot water filters through it to start the brewing process.

Head: the foam on top of beer is a reaction between protein in the malt, compounds in the hops, and carbon dioxide bubbles.

International Bittering Units (IBUs): a standard for measuring the bitterness of beer. It is related to the bitter character of hops. A traditional malty English bitter is normally around 28 IBUs whereas some American IPAs are 70 IBUs or more. If the IBUs are too high, the beer can be unpleasant and hard to drink. The hops will overwhelm the malt flavours.

Kegged beer: Pasteurised and carbonated beer stored and dispensed in pressurised containers called kegs. Bar staff flip a tap open or press a button and the beer pours through tubes from the keg into the glass.

Lager: the other main branch of the beer family tree (ale being the first), lager is made with cool-fermenting yeasts. Lager styles include include Pilsner, Dortmunder and Bock. Lagers are sometimes described as bottom-fermenting beers – a reference to where the yeast cells usually end up in the fermenting vessel. The term 'lager' derives from the German verb '*lagern*', which means 'to store', and refers to the long period of maturation during which authentic lagers are stored in cool conditions for several weeks at low temperatures. This process is sometimes called 'lagering'. Some leading lager brands are made in days rather than months, however, and the beer does not have the same flavour or smooth character.

Lightstruck: some compounds in hops are adversely affected by ultraviolet light and this can alter beer aroma, causing it to smell cheesy, or even like cat wee. In America this problem is known as 'skunky' or 'skunked' beer, as exposure to light can trigger the production of MBT (3-methyl-2-butene-1-thiol), a compound that resembles the noisome defensive odour emitted by skunks. The colour of glass bottles can prevent this issue, e.g. brown glass will block the light. However, some brewing companies prefer to market their beer in green or clear glass because it looks modern and eye-catching. It is possible to use hops that have been modified to remove the compounds that cause the pungency predicament, in which case the beer can be sold in any colour bottle.

Noble hops: a description that describes a group of heritage hops. The term has no official authorisation so any hop could be designated as 'noble' but the definition is usually understood to mean Hallertauer Mittelfrueh, Tettnanger and Spalt from Germany; Saaz from the Czech Republic; Fuggle and Goldings from England.

Original Gravity (OG): a measure of alcohol strength where the solids content of the wort before fermentation is calculated to give the brewer an indication of what the final alcohol level will be. An instrument called a saccharometer, or hydrometer, gauges the density of the wort in comparison to distilled water at 1.000 units. The brewer does some computations to determine what the final gravity, or alcohol level, will be. If, for example, the wort has a density of 1.040, it will have an alcohol level of roughly 4% ABV.

Pasteurisation: named after scientist Louis Pasteur, this is the process of heating beer (and milk and other liquid foods) to prolong its shelf life by inhibiting the growth of spoilage microbes. All kegged and most bottled and canned beer is pasteurised. Pasteurisation does impact on flavour so a brewer that offers pasteurised versions of their cask ale brands will often tweak the recipes slightly by increasing the amount of hops and alcohol level to compensate for what will be lost by heating and filtering the beer.

Phenolic: phenols are chemical compounds widely present in food and drink, where they often contribute flavour and aroma. The most common sources of phenols are yeast and bacteria so many beers can be described as phenolic. Try a wheat beer – those spicy, clove, medicinal and bubblegum characteristics are phenolic.

Real ale: see 'Cask-conditioned ale'.

Reinheitsgebot: also known as the German Beer Purity Law, this was passed in Germany in 1516 to limit brewers in what they could use in beer – only water, malted barley and hops. Yeast was not included in the original law because it was only understood to be an essential constituent of beer in the late seventeenth century. The regulation was replaced in 1993 to permit German brewers to use wheat and sugar. Some brewers still adhere to the Reinheitsgebot and use it as a marketing badge of honour.

Saccharification: the process of breaking down complex carbohydrates (such as the starches in barley malt) into simple sugars.

Skunky: see 'Lightstruck'.

Top fermentation: this refers to the fermentation of ale styles such as bitter, India pale ale and stout. Ale yeast strains normally rise to the top of the fermenting vessel. In this book beer styles are classified as warm (top) or cool (bottom) fermenting beers.

Trub: a term to describe sediment formed during the brewing process. Trub consists of proteins, hops and dead yeast cells and it makes good animal feed.

Warm-fermenting yeast: brewers of ales use a species of yeast known as *Saccharomyces cerevisiae*. It ferments quickly and at a warm temperature of 16–20 °C. This strain often imparts fruity characters in the beer. Beers brewed with *S. cerevisiae* are often called 'top-fermenting', a reference to where most of the yeast cells end up in the vessels after they have fermented the beer. (See also 'Top fermentation'.)

Wort: this is the base of what will become beer and it is produced in a mash tun. It consists of water, and soluble sugars, protein, carbohydrates, colour, and flavour derived from the malted cereal. Wort is boiled with hops in a brewing kettle and then cooled down. Yeast is added to the hoppy wort and the sugars are fermented and convert to alcohol and carbon dioxide.

Yeast: there are more than 1,500 known species of the single-celled fungi called yeast. Brewers use one of several *Saccharomyces* strains, such as *S. cerevisiae, S. pastorianus,* and *S. bayanus. Saccharomyces* is Latin for 'sugar fungus' and during fermentation it eats sugar and converts it to alcohol and carbon dioxide. Most brewers have 'pet' cultured yeasts that are used to ferment all their different brands – meaning that they produce a family of beers connected by the yeast. Some brewers have used the same strain of yeast for decades and these unique microorganisms give the beers an individuality of aroma and flavour. Brewers of Lambic beer do not use cultured yeast strains, instead they rely on wild yeasts that live in the structure of the brewery or the immediate environment.